MALCOLM X: JUSTICE SEEKER

MALCOLM LITTLE

MALCOLM X

EL-HAJJ MALIK EL-SHABAZZ

May 19, 1925 - February 21, 1965

STEPPINGSTONES PRESS

MALCOLM X: JUSTICE SEEKER

I.C.C. LIBRARY

STEPPINGSTONES PRESS

Malcolm X:Justice Seeker
Copyright © 1993 Steppingstones Press
New York, New York 10113-1268

Malcolm X: Justice Seeker is a new edition of a literary tribute published originally in 1983 as part of the journal series of Steppingstones: A Literary Anthology Toward Liberation. The literary material remains the same, the graphics have been modified, and the cover design is new.

Anyone interested in staging or producing the play *The Death of Malcolm X* by Amiri Baraka should contact its author and literary agent to obtain permission.

All inquiries should be addressed to:
Steppingstones Press
Box 1268
New York, New York 10113-1268
(212) 691-2457
Fax: (212) 727-3937

ISBN: 0-935821-01-5
(Originally published as ISSN: 0735-4789 - 1983)

Cover design by Pennebaker Design, Houston, TX

Printed in the United States of America.

ACKNOWLEDGEMENTS

I am grateful for the contributions of the authors included in this collection.

I wish to express my gratitude to Amiri Baraka, Gwendolyn Brooks, John Henrik Clarke, and Sonia Sanchez, for permission to reprint their works; *The Death of Malcolm X*, by Amiri Baraka, from *New Plays from the Black Theatre*, (New York: Bantam Books, 1969), Ed Bullins (Editor); to Harper & Row Publishers for permission to reprint the poem "Malcolm X," by Ms. Brooks from the book *The World of Gwendolyn Brooks*, © 1971 Gwendolyn Brooks Blakely; portions of the essay by John Henrik Clarke, which appears in the "Introduction" to *Malcolm X: The Man and His Times*, (New York: Macmillan, 1969); for the poems by Ms. Sanchez, "Malcolm," and "For Unborn Malcolms," reprinted from *Homecoming*, (Detroit: Broadside Press, 1969). The poem by D.H. Melhem is from a collection of poetry, *Poems for Poets/Poems for You*, published in 1983.

I thank Ademola Olugebefola, for his artistic contribution to the original issue of the literary tribute, and for the additional graphics provided for this new edition. Also, I thank Haesun Kim Lerch and David Lerch of Pennebaker Design for the cover of this book, and Ward Pennebaker for his continued creative support and friendship. And finally, my greatest gratitude to my friends and family who are unmentioned but are much loved.

The collages by Ademola are titled as follows: *Big Red* (p. 7); *X is the Constant* (p. 11); *Solitude* (p. 14); *Think* (p. 29); *All The Children* (p. 30); *Cool Breeze* (p. 59); *Leader* (p. 80); *Heavy Rappin* (p. 109); and *Stop the Clan* (p. 110).

FOREWORD

I am proud and honored to reissue this literary tribute to Malcolm X, the Justice Seeker. The writings and art work are insightful, poignant, and powerful. The strength and durability of Malcolm X's beliefs led to the new title for the tribute, and the new cover art work is intended to reflect this focus. This collection of reprinted and new poems, essays and a play are a means of shedding light on, and sharing admiration for a great man. Intended to complement other works, this tribute stands on its own as originally published.

There are many works that should be explored in discovering the essence and power of Malcolm X as a leader, thinker and man. *The Autobiography of Malcolm X*, edited by Alex Haley (Grove Press) is one of the important works of literature in our time. It is a compelling and riveting narrative of one man's attempt to overcome a world vanquished by chaos and injustice. *Malcolm X: The Man and His Times*, edited by John Henrik Clarke (Macmillan); *The Life and Death of Malcolm X* by Peter Goldman (Harper & Row); *The Last Year of Malcolm X* by George Breitman (Pathfinder Press), and scores of articles written on him, as well as his published speeches and manuscripts serve as a core in understanding his dynamism and complexity.

If we examine and analyze these writings, we can derive some perspective on issues that must still be resolved. Political action on the local level was extremely important to Malcolm X, yet at the time of his death he had become an internationalist. He was concerned about the oppression met by people of color, and the liberation struggles around the world.

Can it be said that the conditions in Africa of chaos, drought, famine, pestilence, war and apartheid are all accidents? As the new world order is being assembled, who will speak for the weak? Who will ensure that nations that are not industrial or

military powers are equal members of the global village?

Malcolm X embodies four concepts to be explored: change, responsibility, action, and the pursuit of excellence. Change and evolution were the keystones to Malcolm X's success. To be able to climb from the bottom to the top, spiritually, physically, intellectually, and fearlessly is the marvel. The catalyst itself was knowledge which nurtured his energies and efforts as a liberator.

To sustain change toward a goal takes a sense of responsibility, for oneself, one's family, one's community. Such responsible change can only be carried out through action, with a passion for excellence.

In a nation and world that is in the throes of change, renewed guidance from Malcolm X's words and actions become steps toward achieving a just and peaceful world.

James B. Gwynne
Editor
November 10, 1992
New York City

TABLE OF CONTENTS

9

ESSAYS

INTRODUCTION

"I think that Malcolm X was the greatest gift in this century. And he did it by his own strengths. It makes what I have to do in raising six children look very easy. I had the example there to follow, long before I had to walk the same road." These are the words of Mrs. Betty Shabazz a few years ago in an interview with Denise Crittendon in Chicago.

In a lecture at the Countee Cullen Library in November of 1981, Gil Noble, an award-winning journalist, spoke on "Malcolm X: An Era And His Legacy." He stated that "Malcolm was one of the most significant lives that ever occurred in history. Malcolm is a deep river. He is not a shallow stream. He is not easy to understand. He is still running far ahead of us. He is the most courageous man of this or any time." And he added: "Malcolm went to the lowest element of our people and picked out the gold nuggets."

Mrs. Shabazz has said that "Malcolm was never a racist. That was part of the press invention. To point out the injustice done to minorities is not to say you are a racist or a racist in reverse." And "If he (Malcolm X) had lived, the world would not be as it is today, because for the longest time, he was the conscience of America."

These words provide some ways of looking at Malcolm X (El Hajj Malik el-Shabazz) as a man whose place in history is unsettled only as we are unwilling to comprehend the parameters of his questions and their answers, and act on them.

The story of his life, development and growth, and evidence that Malcolm X was a man of change, as well as for change, have been outlined with honesty and boldness in the *Autobiography*. Phases of his life are well known, from an early childhood crushed by the cruelty of racism, to the fast life that crashed into the hell of prison, the conversion and transformation as a Black Muslim, to the brief and dynamic moments of the last months of his life. There have been many attempts to distort his views, especially on subjects such as self-help, self-defense, or even education. The nearly two decades since his death have provided us with many lessons; on questions of race, political strategies, and other issues, his answers are still on the mark. Malcolm X was a man of reality. He knew quite well the dimensions of the problem, yet he still believed that change could occur in this country.

The plight of millions of Black people, and people of color throughout the world, mired in lives of destitution, humiliation, and oppression, solely because of their skin color, became the focus of his life: calling attention to and for the end of it. This idea was radical in concept and action - it would be the cause of his death. His legacy is of a man committed to action, against injustice, willing to sacrifice his all.

Malcolm X's perspective was international: he saw connections with everything in the world. Where injustice reigns, the struggle for freedom, human dignity and self-determination must and will go on. He offers inspiration to the souls of Black people, and to any one involved in a struggle against oppression and exploitation. We can draw solace from the spirit of Malcolm X. He showed us the power of the individual and the purpose of community.

As a man, husband and father, activist and friend, his was a liberating spirit. The same kind of honesty in dealing with the problems that beset our country and the world is needed today. The answers must be as forthright as the analysis, and must be rooted in action for change. It is what we do with the time we have left that will make the difference.

James B. Gwynne
New York City, 1983

POETRY

MALCOLM X

For Dudley Randall

Original.
Ragged-round.
Rich-robust.

He had the hawk-man's eyes.
We gasped. We saw the maleness.
The maleness raking out and making guttural the air
and pushing us to walls.

And in a soft and fundamental hour
a sorcery devout and vertical
beguiled the world.

He opened us—
who was a key,

who was a man.

Gwendolyn Brooks

17

FOR BLACK POETS
WHO THINK OF LEADERSHIP

By song
through preacher
political
through field of hands and hearts
raising like wheat
the swords that are ploughshares
the faces that Malcolm saw
that Malcolm touched
with the colored strands
of his final vision

Black poets:
you enact the deep heroic line

D.H. Melhem

A LIBATIONARY CHANT-PRAYER
FOR MALCOLM
AND HIS SACRED AUTOBIOGRAPHY

Ancestor Malcolm
We pause periodically to acknowledge you and your
Holy text
With liquid and scents
May your life-words work us
May we live your later-life now
May your life be the image we seek to realize
May your spirit impregnate our results
May you fire our actions, that we may give
Birth to your vision

Again, we pause to center ourselves, to remember
Your ways and wisdom, to renew and relive
Your initial impact on our lives

Please accept this
Offering

Louis C. Young, Jr.

MALCOLM

do not speak to me of martyrdom
of men who die to be remembered
on some parish day.

 i don't believe in dying
though i too shall die
and violets like castanets
will echo me.

yet this man
this dreamer,
thick-lipped with words
will never speak again
and in each winter
when the cold air cracks
with frost, i'll breathe
his breath and mourn
my gun-filled nights.
he was the sun that tagged
the western sky and
melted tiger-scholars
while they searched for stripes.
he said, "fuck you white
man. we have been
curled too long. nothing
is sacred now. not your

white faces nor any
land that separates
until some voices
squat with spasms."

do not speak to me of living.
life is obscene with crowds
of white on black.
death is my pulse.
what might have been
is not for him/or me
but what could have been
floods the womb until i drown.

Sonia Sanchez

FOR UNBORN MALCOLMS

git the word out
now.
  to the man/boy
taking a holiday
from murder.
  tell him
we hip to his shit and that
the next time he kills one
of our
  blk/princes
          some of his faggots
gonna die
  a stone/cold/death.
                  yeah.
it's time.
  an eye for an eye
  a tooth for a tooth
  don't worry bout his balls
they al
  ready gone.
          git the word
out that us blk/niggers
          are out to lunch
and the main course
is gonna be his white meat.
                  yeah.

Sonia Sanchez

REQUIEM FOR MALCOLM X

You are Malcolm X
Born Malcolm Little
Alias Home Boy
Alias Big Red
Alias Brother Malcolm
Alias Malik Shabazz.
And
You are dead. Quite dead
Shot down in the Audubon Ballroom
The day before Washington's Birthday
The day you were to name the men
You said were set upon your trail
To try to do you in
Now you are dead
Shot down in The Audubon Ballroom
Late Sunday afternoon.

Tell it not in Gath
Publish it not in the streets of Askelon
Lest the daughters of the Philistines rejoice
Lest the daughters of the uncircumcised triumph!

You are Malcolm X
A man destined for tragedy
A man who lived on the edge of violence
A man never reconciled
To your society
Or to your condition
Or to yourself
A man of tortuous emotions

Of violent personal conflicts
A man of impossible yearnings
A black man who wanted
to be a man
In America
And now you are dead.
Dead.

In you, Brother Malcolm
In you, Malik Shabazz
The irresistible force
Met the immovable object
And you are dead.

Brother Malcolm, you were born dead!

There was a bullet made for you
A bullet with your name
Etched in blood
Made the same hour
You quit your mother's womb
Screaming your intent
To be a man
In this man's
America.

C. Eric Lincoln

X...IS A CONSTANT IN TIME...

I've got to be
  the first person in my family
    to be free
        will you help me
        Malcolm X
        with your memory?

'Cause we too soon forget
  the barbaric neglect
    we get in this country
        everyday
        can I say you're with me
        Malcolm X?

May I tell my son you wouldn't run
  when oppression thrust its
    horrid, ancient head in your face
        may we try to keep pace
        with you
        Malcolm X?

And I know you did your homework and
  learned your lessons well
    when the palefaced liars said
        we came, with tails, from hell
        can you show me how they
        cut theirs, Malcolm X?

I see you followed the Creator
　　and not the one that's blind
　　　　to all the pain and suffering
　　　　　　　they inflict upon my mind
　　　　　　　won't ya help me
　　　　　　　ease the pressure, Malcolm X?

And when you spoke the only truth
　　as you always did
　　　　the ones who could not stand it
　　　　　　　had to stop it
　　　　　　　nailed the lid
　　　　　　　air-tight upon your coffin

willing truth be still
　　but the truth cannot be
　　　　silenced
　　　　　　　you've got to guide
　　　　　　　to keep the will
　　　　　　　Malcolm X.

Malcolm X: come back
　　Malcolm X: be heard
　　　　By the teachings of the living
　　　　　　keep on giving us the word.

                                J.E.M. Jones

IN HONOR OF TRUTH AND
THE PROPHET MALCOLM X

And there came to us
a prophet
who, with words and deeds like fire,
burned away the waxing pretensions
of the modern era.
And his fire did not only burn,
it warmed and gave light.
And he arose from among the people,
and the places they knew.
He was of the people,
so that none could say,
"there is one who is unlike us,
one who does not know our suffering."
And he spoke brazenly, by virtue of the truth;
for in that time, as now, the truth
was held in no esteem.
He awakened the invaluable remembrance:
we are Africans, ancient and renown
Many would hear and love themselves
and each other.
Many knew and sensed the greatness,
the antiquity of Ethiopia,
the splendor of Egypt,
the wealth of Ghana,
the might of the Congo.
From Kings and Queens to slaves
without name or place, to ex-slaves
without name or place of remembrance.
What sharp-edged truth, unmindful of favor,
which was his burden to convey, who taught us

not so much to tell what would be,
but to tell rightly what was and is.
The prophet Malcolm X, died as he lived:
in giving of himself.
Those who knew him, even those
who never met him (yet knew him),
were not dismayed at his physical passing.
His legacy was forged of spirit,
set to pass the trial of time.
Those who value the truth,
the hard and real truth,
honor him and others who came like him.
And for as long as truth remains truth,
which for us is forever
the spirit of Malcolm X,
the spirit of a free Africa
burns bright, scorching as needed
and giving warmth
and giving light.

Juan Villegas

ESSAYS

THE MEANING OF
EL-HAJJ MALIK EL-SHABAZZ IN THE 1980'S

James Jennings

Let me say, first of all, that it is both an honor and a pleasure for me to be here tonight; I especially wish to thank the Black Students Association for inviting me to say a few words concerning the meaning of Malcolm X's life for all of us in the 1980's.

Unfortunately, in recent years we have moved away from these kinds of important educational gatherings; we have not sponsored enough activities to commemorate and to study those Black men and women who made conscious decisions to sacrifice their lives, and their families in order to make it possible for Black students to be at a place like Harvard University's Kennedy School of Government. We are here as a direct consequence of the sacrifices made by Malcolm X and others like him. We represent an extension of Malcolm X's life and struggles; we are part—an integral part—of the historical and social processes which saw Malcolm X rise from a petty criminal in the streets of Detroit and Boston, to one of the most respected and feared Black human beings in the entire history of this country. To deny this is to deny history, and it is to belittle the individual and collective struggles of Black people for mere survival in America.

When I say that we owe our presence here to Malcolm X, it does not mean that he was a member of one of Harvard University's admissions committees; but Malcolm X did force the most powerful institutions in this country to expose their long colonial and hypocritical relationships with the Black community. By choosing to speak freely Malcolm X forced the holders and managers of wealth to at least consider, to reassess, the style of oppresssion against Black people in the United States. As a result of the Black protest movement which Malcolm X helped to spark and sustain, colleges and universities which had not allowed even a handful of Blacks into their hallowed halls, began to accept—albeit grudgingly—a few more Black and Third World students into their lily-white classsrooms. Whether Black students think they agree or disagree with this man's philosophy and politics, you should at least consider that in some ways you did benefit from Malcolm X's struggles against racism, classism and sexism. It is wholly illogical to assume that higher education in this country, which had insisted on lily-white classrooms for many, many generations, all of a sudden saw the light in the mid-sixties and decided to mend their racist ways. No! What caused some degree of change were the words and deeds of people unafraid to speak the truth as they saw it.

Understanding Malcolm X's life and death is a crucial tool for your intellectual development as well as for your social and psychological survival. An appreciation of Malcolm X's life and philosophy and how this philosophy changed over a relatively short period of time—can serve as an intellectual guidepost in your struggles to leave this institution with your mind and soul intact. It can also assist you in understanding your society as you enter into it with your B.A.'s and B.S.'s! It may help you to make decisions affecting your lives and the future of those around you.

There are three ways in which I would like to try to illustrate the significance of Malcolm X in the eighties; there is first, an historical dimension. There is also an intellectual and social level at which we may discuss this topic.

Historically, Malcolm X is important to you because he is the first Black leader in America to represent and lead a mass movement within a revolutionary framework of political action. Without minimizing the significance of Marcus Garvey and the Hon. Elijah Muhammed, we must recognize that Malcolm X took us a step further. I think that this is what made him the most feared man in American history. Malcolm sent shock waves through America with his messages; in response to this various powerful interests tried a number of ways by which to attack him, ultimately resulting in his assassination. The FBI carried out an active and officially sanctioned program to discourage the emergence and growth of Black organizations based on Malcolm X's philosophy; this government agency also tried to dissuade what were considered 'moderate' Black leaders from adopting the ideas of Malcolm X. There were special attempts to prevent Black youth and Black students especially, from even looking at the philosophy of Malcolm X. And there was good reason for this kind of response on the part of the U.S. Government. In a memo issued by J. Edgar Hoover to FBI field personnel on August 25, 1967 he urged agents to harass and disrupt any Black militant group which was attracting Black youths to its ranks. Why? Why is it so important to keep you from understanding the ideas of Malcolm X? Why is this very talk here tonight a threat to certain people in this country and in this very University? Malcolm X represented a new kind of Black leader. He was someone who refused to think and operate within a political framework which did not question the structural position of Black people in the U.S. His framework called for new kinds of power arrangements; it called for challenges to the kinds of values which allow us to put profits in front of people. In that Blacks are the most oppressed nationality in American society, it is especially important for those concerned with the political stability to keep such ideas from this sector. If Black youth are allowed to study and discuss the ideas of Malcolm X the consequences could be dangerous from the perspective of those who hold power and wealth in our society.

Another important contribution which Malcolm X made to you was the development of logical and analytical approaches to social and political problems facing Blacks. Malcolm X was a lucid thinker. It is interesting how some observers have portrayed Malcolm X; they say that he was emotional; they are beginning to say that he was a bit psychotic; they have dismissed him as just another angry, loud Black man. Yet Malcolm X was one of the clearest political and social thinkers in American history. Malcolm X provided to us analytical tools, via the ideas which he discussed, by which to understand unfolding domestic and international events affecting our lives. While the so-called intellectuals in government and academic positions were busy glorifying and bragging about American democracy—and in very emotional terms—Malcolm X was providing insight. He offered concrete analysis in his discussion about the Black rebellions beginning to sweep the U.S. in the early sixties and cataclysmic international developments. I would urge you, while a student here, to compare carefully the thoughts and writings of Malcolm X with some of his intellectual contemporaries. You will discover that it was he who was the scholar; the 'established' and 'credentialed' scholars were, for the most part, the emotional ones.

I know that some of you will scoff at the idea of this once petty criminal, with little formal education, in fact being the intellectual superior to the academicians you have been taught to idolize (and many times not because of their ideas, but rather as a result of their positions). And no matter how interested and sincere some of you might be about understanding the world today, you will not bother to study Malcolm X seriously because your professors may not sanction it; perhaps some of you feel that unless the *New York Times* or *Newsweek* says so, it really isn't very important to you. But listen to me: by continuing to reject the intellectual importance and significance of Malcolm X you are bound to make the same kinds of stupid errors made by other scholars on the payroll of the powerful in American society. Let me give you an example of what I am trying to describe to you. And let me begin this example by citing an established newspaper which, of course, you all respect and read. Recently the *Boston Globe* provided a series of articles on political developments in the country of Iran. One article, titled "Embassy Papers: No Hint of Islam" (2/5/82), reported that,

> In all the hundreds of pages of U.S. embassy documents captured in Teheran and released by Islamic students, representing years of detailed analysis of Iranian society, there is hardly a glimmer of the possibility of a religiously-inspired revolution.

Imagine this! American intellectuals, with all their money, university positions, publications and so forth, were not able to sense what was happening in Iranian society. When the Ayatollah Khomeini wrested power from the Shah the intellectuals working for the U.S. State Department and CIA were caught by surprise. This is similar to the state of shock these same intellectuals found themselves in when racial explosions rocked the country in cities across the United States. Malcolm X, however, foresaw a wave of racial protest in the ghettos of America because of his steadfastness in approaching social and political problems analytically. This is all to suggest that learning should be as broadly based as possible. You cannot comprehend what is occurring around you by relying solely on the tools you obtain at places like Harvard University. Malcolm X did not attend Harvard, he didn't have a Ph.D or even a B.A. But he was still an intellectual giant because of his insistence on true scholarship. This is the kind of scholarship that is not shackled by credentials or acceptable ideas; it is a free scholarship—based on an honest pursuit of Truth. If ever you are confused about this, or if ever you are not sure how to approach certain social and political questions, don't be afraid or ashamed to look at Malcolm X. His thoughts and writings, collectively, provide a rigorous standard of intellectual inquiry.

Malcolm X also has meaning to you because he developed a framework by which this society could become a truly democratic one—politically, economically, and culturally. Every significant Black leader involved in the struggles for civil and human rights has gravitated in varying degrees towards Malcolm X's philosophy. Blacks with diverse ideological predispositions have moved towards Malcolm X and his ideas. Martin Luther King was assassinated at the point which he begins to embrace the ideas of Malcolm X. I would urge you to read his work *Where Do We Go From Here* (1967), and a more recent piece by Manning Marable, "Towards An Understanding of Martin Luther King" for additional information on this point. If you wish to understand the viability or validity of any proposal, any strategy or program with the goal of uplifting Black people, you too will have to study Malcolm X. He provided answers to many of our questions.

Finally, let me say that Malcolm X has an important spiritual meaning for you, today. Malcolm X was a model human being. In her essay, "Malcolm X As A Husband and A Father," Betty Shabazz describes him as a devout and strong family man. He was an honest person. As strongly as he held to his convictions he did not believe in forcing them upon anyone. He didn't drink or smoke. He loved his children. One of his closest associates and friends for many years, Minister Louis Farrakhan, tells us that Malcolm X's personal code of ethics almost made him superior to those around him. He was a patient and warm individual. In today's world, any person who can be so described demands our attention. I would like to end this presentation on this 'spiritual' note—among all of us in this auditorium, it could very well be the most important thing to be said of Malcolm X. I'd like to do this by reading a short passage from his eulogy delivered by Ossie Davis on February 27, 1965 at the Faith Temple Church of God in Harlem:

...Many will ask what Harlem finds to honor in this stormy controversial and bold young captain—and we will smile.

Many will say turn away—away from this man, for he is not a man but a demon, a monster, a subverter and an enemy of the Black man—and we will smile.

And we will answer and say unto them: Did you ever talk to Brother Malcolm? Did you ever touch him, or have him smile at you? Did you ever really listen to him? Did he ever do a mean thing? Was he ever himself associated with violence or any public disturbance? For if you did you would know him: Malcolm was our manhood, our living, Black manhood! This was his meaning to his people. And, in honoring him we honor the best in ourselves.

*****

Presentation made at the "Malcolm X Weekend," Harvard University - The John F. Kennedy School of Government, February 19, 1982. Sponsored and organized by the Black Students Association, Harvard University.

MALCOLM X: THE MAN AND HIS TIMES

John Henrik Clarke

To place Malcolm X and his roughhewn grandeur in proper perspective, one must first understand the nature of the society that produced him and ultimately destroyed him. To a large extent, the shadow of slavery still hangs over this land, and affects the daily life of every American. Slavery was the black gold that produced America's first wealth and power. Slavery was the breeding ground for the most contagious and contaminating monster of all time—racism.

It was this racism and oppression by white America that convinced Malcolm X of the necessity of Black nationalism as the vehicle for Black liberation, as opposed to "integration," while he was in the Black Muslim movement. Although his Black nationalism, while he was in the Muslim organization, was narrow and sectarian, this did not prevent him from playing a tremendously important role in the evolution of the Black freedom struggle.

Prior to the arrival of Malcolm X on the scene, most of white America looked upon the established civil rights organizations as "extremist," although most of them were creatures and creations of the white controllers of power. But Malcolm came along and said, "Not only do I refuse to integrate with you, white man, but I demand that I be completely separated from you in some states of our own or back home in Africa; not only is your Christianity a fraud but your 'democracy' a brittle lie." Neither the white man nor his Black apologists could answer the latter argument.

Because they could not answer Malcolm in this area, they attacked him where he was most vulnerable—the concept of separatism and that all white folks were "blue-eyed devils"— labeling him a "hatemonger," "racist," "dangerous fanatic," "Black supremacist," etc. In reality, he was none of these

things.   Certainly he didn't preach "Black supremacy."
Malcolm X preached Black pride, Black redemption, Black
reaffirmation, and he gave the Black woman the image of a
Black man that she could respect.

The fact that Malcolm X, while in the Black Muslim
movement, could reject a white person on any terms caused
most of white America psychological turmoil. And instilled
admiration and pride in most Black Americans. For the egos
of most white Americans are so bloated that they cannot
conceive of a Black man rejecting them.

It can be stated categorically that Malcolm X, while in the
Black Muslim movement and out of it, created the present
stage of the civil rights struggle—to the effect that he was a
catalytic agent—offstage, sarcastically criticizing the "civil
rights leaders," popping a whip which activated them into
more radical action and programs.   He was the alternative
which the power holders of America had to deal with, if they
didn't deal with the established "civil rights leaders."

On December 1, 1963, shortly after President Kennedy's
assassination, Malcolm X addressed a public rally at Manhat-
tan Center in New York City.   He was speaking as a replace-
ment for Elijah Muhammad as he had done many times before.
After the speech, during a question and answer period, Malcolm
X made the remark that led to his suspension as a Muslim
minister.   In answer to a question, "What do you think about
President Kennedy's assassination?" Malcolm X answered
that he saw the case as "The chickens coming home to roost."
Soon after the remark, Malcolm X was suspended by Elijah
Muhammad and directed to stop speaking for ninety days.
After some weeks, when Malcolm X realized that there were
a number of highly placed persons in the Black Muslim
movement conspiring against him, seemingly with Elijah
Muhammad's consent, he left the movement.

He devotes a chapter in his book (*The Autobiography of
Malcolm X*) to the growth of his disenchantment and eventual

suspension from the Black Muslim movement. He says:

> I had helped Mr. Muhammad and his ministers to
> revolutionize the American Black man's thinking, open-
> ing his eyes until he would never look again in the same
> fearful way at the white man... If I harbored any
> personal disappointment whatsoever, it was that pri-
> vately I was convinced that our Nation of Islam could be
> an even greater force in the American Black man's
> overall struggle—if we engaged in more action. By that
> I mean I thought privately that we should have amended,
> or relaxed, our general non-engagement policy. I felt
> that, wherever Black people committed themselves, in
> the Little Rocks and the Birminghams and other places,
> militantly disciplined Muslims should also be there—for
> all the world to see, and respect and discuss.

On March 8, 1964, he publicly announced that he was
starting a new organization. In fact two new organizations
were started, the Muslim Mosque, Inc., and the Organization
of Afro-American Unity.

Malcolm X was still somewhat beholden to Elijah
Muhammad in the weeks immediately following his break
with the movement. At his press conference on March 12, he
said in part:

> I am and always will be a Muslim. My religion is
> Islam. I still believe that Mr. Muhammad's analysis
> of the problem is the most realistic, and that his
> solution is the best one. This means that I too believe
> the best solution is complete separation, with our
> people going back home, to our own African home-
> land. But separation back to Africa is still a long-
> range program, and while it is yet to materialize, 22
> million of our people who are still here in America

need better food, clothing, housing, education, and jobs right now. Mr. Muhammad's program does point us back homeward, but it also contains within it what we could and should be doing to help solve many of our problems while we are still here.

Internal differences within the Nation of Islam forced me out of it. I did not leave of my own free will. But now that it has happened I intend to make the most of it. Now that I have more independence of action, I intend to use a more flexible approach toward working with others to get a solution to this problem. I do not pretend to be a divine man, but I do believe in divine guidance, divine power, and in the fulfillment of divine prophecy. I am not educated, nor am I an expert in any particular field...but I am sincere and my sincerity is my credential.

The problem facing our people here in America is bigger than other personal or organizational differences. Therefore, as leaders, we must stop worrying about the threat that we seem to think we pose to each other's personal prestige, and concentate our united efforts toward solving the unending hurt that is being done daily to our people here in America.

I am going to organize and head a new Mosque in New York City, known as the Muslim Mosque, Inc. This gives us a religious base, and the spiritual force necessary to rid our people of the vices that destroy the moral fiber of our community.

Our political philosophy will be Black nationalism. Our economic and social philosophy will be Black nationalism. Our cultural emphasis will be Black nationalism.

Many of our people aren't religiously inclined, so the Muslim Mosque, Inc. will be organized in such a manner as to provide for the active participation of all Negroes in our political, economic, and social programs, despite their religious or non-religious beliefs.

The political philosophy of Black nationalism means: We must control the politics and the politicians of our community. They must no longer take orders from outside forces. We will organize and sweep out of office all Negro politicians who are puppets for the outside forces.

Malcolm X had now thrust himself into a new area of conflict that would take him, briefly, to a high point of international attention and partial acceptance. During the last phase of his life Malcolm X established this Muslim Mosque, Inc., and the non-religious Organization of Afro-American Unity, patterned after the Organization of African Unity. He attempted to internationalize the civil rights struggle by taking it to the United Nations.

In several trips to Africa and one to Mecca, he sought the counsel and support of African and Asian heads of state. His trip to Mecca and Africa had a revolutionary effect upon his thinking. His perennial call had always been for black unity and self-defense in opposition to the "integrationist's" program of nonviolence, passive resistance, and "Negro-white unity." When he returned home from his trip he was no longer opposed to progressive whites uniting with revolutionary Blacks, as his enemies would suggest. But to Malcolm, and correctly so, the role of the white progressive was not in Black organizations but in white organizations in white communities, convincing and converting the unconverted to the Black cause. Further, and perhaps more important, Malcolm had observed the perfidy of the white liberal and the American Left whenever Afro-Americans sought to be instruments of their own liberation. He was convinced that there could be no Black-white unity until there was Black unity; that there could be no workers' solidarity until there was racial solidarity.

The overwhelming majority of white America demonstrates daily that they cannot and will not accept the Black man as an equal in all the ramifications of this acceptance—after having three hundred and forty-five years of racism preached to them from the pulpit, taught in the primer and textbook, practiced by the government, apotheosized on editorial pages, lauded on the airways and television screens. It would be tantamount to self-castration, a gutting of the ego. It would be asking white America completely to purge itself of everything it has been taught, fed, and has believed for three hundred and forty-five years.

It was this recognition of what racism had done to the white man and to the mind of the Black man that the following paragraph was and is a keystone of the Organization of Afro-American Unity's program:

> We must revamp our entire thinking and redirect our learning trends so that we can put forth a confident identity and wipe out the false image built up by an oppressive society. We can build a foundation for liberating our minds by studying the different philosophies and psychologies of others. Provisions are being made for the study of languages of Eastern origin such as Swahili, Hausa, and Arabic. Such studies will give us, as Afro-Americans, a direct access to ideas and history of our ancestors, as well as histories of mankind at large.

More so than any other Afro-American leader, Malcolm X realized that there must be a concomitant cultural and educational revolution if the physical revolution is to be successful. No revolution has ever sustained itself on emotion. When Malcolm X returned from his trip to Mecca and Africa, he completely repudiated the Black Muslims' program of separation, their acquisitive thirst for money and property and machine idolatry. He felt that they were merely imitating the racist enemy. He still believed in separation from his racist enemy, but his was an ideological separation. To Malcolm X, the Afro-American must transcend his enemy, not imitate him. For he foresaw that both the Black Muslims and the "integrationists" were aping the oppressor; that neither recognized that the struggle for Black freedom was neither social nor moral. It was and is a power struggle; a struggle between the white haves and the Black have-nots. A struggle of the oppressor and the oppressed. And if the oppressed is to breach the power of the oppressor, he must either acquire power or align himself with power.

Therefore, it is not accidental that Malcolm's political arm, the Organization of Afro-American Unity, was patterned to the letter and spirit after the Organization of African Unity. Nor should it be surprising that he officially linked up the problems of Afro-Americans with the problems of his Black brothers and sisters on the mother continent. Malcolm X's vision was broad enough to see that the Afro-Americans were not a "minority" as the enemy and his lackeys would have us believe. Afro-Americans are not an isolated 25 million. There are over 100 million Black people in the Western Hemisphere—Cuba, Brazil, Latin America, the West Indies, North America, etc. Malcolm knew that when we unite these millions with the 300 million on the African continent the Black man becomes a mighty force. The second largest people on earth. And so Malcolm's perennial theme was unity, unity, unity.

The formation of the Organization of Afro-American Unity and the establishment of an official connection with Africa was one of the most important acts of the twentieth century. For this act gave the Afro-Americans an official link with the new emerging power emanating from both Africa and Asia. Thus, Malcolm X succeeded where Marcus Garvey and others had failed. Doing this, Malcolm projected the cause of Afro-American freedom into the international arena of power.

When he internationalized the problem, by raising it from the level of civil rights to that of human rights and by linking up with Africa, Malcolm X threw himself into the cross fire of that invisible, international cartel of power and finance which deposes presidents and prime ministers, dissolves parliaments, if they refuse to do their bidding. It was this force, I believe, that killed Malcolm X, that killed Lumumba, that killed Hammarskjold.

There is another and more potent reason why the American oppressors feared Malcolm X and desired him dead. And that is the publicized fact that he was going to bring the oppression of Afro-Americans before the United Nations, charging the United States Government with genocide. Many of the oppressors had conniptions when confronted with the prospect of a world body discussing the problems of Afro-Americans.

In the introduction to Malcolm X's autobiography, M.S. Handler has said: "No man in our time aroused fear and hatred in the white man as did Malcolm, because in him the white man sensed an implacable foe who could not be had for any price—a man unreservedly committed to the cause of liberating the Black man in American society rather than integrating the Black man into that society."

He was, more precisely, a man in search of a definition of himself and his relationship to his people, his country, and the world. That a man who had inhabited the "lower depths" of life could rise in triumph as a reproach to its ills, and become an uncompromising champion of his people, is in itself a remarkable feat. Malcolm X went beyond this feat. Though he came from the American ghetto and directed his message to the people in the American ghetto first of all, he also became, in his brief lifetime, a figure of world importance. He was assassinated on February 25, 1965, while on the threshold of his potential.

About the men of his breed, the writer John Oliver Killens has said: "He was a dedicated patriot: Dignity was his country, Manhood was his government and Freedom was his land."

FOR MALCOLM, FOR US

Kalamu ya Salaam

Where are our real leaders now
Where, the pride bearers
   hope inspirers
The spokespeople
   perceptive articulaters
The guides
   keen compasses
The thinkers
   reality analyzers
Where are today's Malcolms?
In which of us
   does his spirit rise?

El Hajj Malik el-Shabazz is prominently displayed in the front room of our home directly above a large, Garvey-inspired red, black and green liberation flag. Although I believe Malcolm deserves such a place of honor, I am not unaware that King and Kennedy traditionally occupy revered spots above mantlepieces and on walls in the homes of most African-Americans who display the image of a national leader.

But unlike Kennedy who was rich, white and a president of the United States or King who was economically secure, college educated and a baptist minister, Malcolm represented neither the masters nor the house negroes. Malcolm was clearly cut from the stock of field slaves. Blazingly so, irreversibly so.

Although the majority of us can be seduced by an equal opportunity, there are exceptional men and women, like Malcolm, who are different drummers. These stalwarts are not establishment celebrated and decorated drum majors leading us in main street protests and parades, but African-oriented maroon master drummers calling us to the hills. Like Cabral said of Guinea-Bissau, in the flatlands of these metropolitan American ghettoes, "our people are our hills." And, oh, how much so many of us hate to climb.

***

Black fingers on the trigger
Black blood on the floor
When they call for assassins
Too often Black men answer.

Bilal was busted in Belize, a small country in Central America. You remember Bilal, he played tenor with Gil Scott-Heron. The media flashed FBI-supplied mug shots across the country. You remember Fulani. Fulani and Bilal were one. And she and her children coolly faced the hired guns who came to arrest them at dawn across a Mississippi field with helicopters and bullhorns, and rifle barrels trained on the small wood frame home. The law enforcers, 1980 paddy-rollers, slave catchers in three button suits, shuffled Fulani in and out of jail and demanded that she talk to them. Fulani defied them. Bilal eluded them. Eventually, underground, Bilal and Fulani reunited, quietly, with low profile, near the ocean.

Like Malcolm, Bilal and Fulani were betrayed by those who cloaked their treason in the Black mantle of solidarity. Their helping hands were just another link in the chain. Remember the name Babatunde Ahmed, a.k.a. James Tucker. It was he, along with another "brother," Lloyd "Rip" Lazard, who went to Belize and came back publicly trumpeting his mission to raise money for Fulani and Bilal. He said they had asked him to do it. Four days or so later Bilal was busted. And from jail a few weeks ago Fulani called: Babatunde was lying, no one asked him to do anything.

Is it only the psychology of oppression that leads us to finger each other? But just as Bilal and Fulani have survived this treachery, in a similar way, although he is dead, Malcolm survived his own murder. Long after those who shot him are forgotten, Malcolm will live because we will remember him not with street signs and wall posters, but with deeds flung defiantly back into the teeth of our oppressors like a runaway smashing a bloodhound's skull with a rock. Malcolm survives because we remember, and motivated by the memory, we act. Thus, Malcolm's memory serves us well.

***

Malcolm learned
to read
in jail
while we
on the outside
continue
to watch
television

Two of Malcolm's books are classics of our national literature: *The Autobiography of Malcolm X* and *Malcolm X on Afro-American History.*

His autobiography is done in the oral history/slave narrative mode, a mode favored in African-American literature. Malcolm's story was the story of an era and an awakening. Malcolm's father, a Garveyite, defined Malcolm's birth in struggle. Malcolm's middle period: one of lumpen anti-social defiance; hustling to survive, but essentially living off the flesh of the less fortunate. Malcolm did not disguise this reactionary behavior in shrouds of lumpen-revolutionary rhetoric a la Eldridge Cleaver, but instead dissected it as a sickness, a death state really, from which he had to be cured and raised. And finally, the moment of the sixties: he overturned himself and became our main man on the scene. Malcolm went toe to toe with our enemies whether on their turf from the podium at Harvard University or on his own from step ladders in the streets of Harlem.

His history book is a groundation which prepares us to appreciate our history, and indeed, appreciate history as a whole. "It is impossible to understand the present or prepare for the future unless we have some knowledge of the past." Surely we are now in need of understanding and preparation.

A thorough examination of Malcolm's life and writings are essential for us the living. His books are required reading for our vital education.

We need to understand what moved him from the zombie state of lumpen hustling to the defiant path of liberator. We need to learn how this man became our martyr. We must fully appreciate the extensive machinations of our oppressors, and the story of state destruction of Malcolm is particularly instructive in this regard. Finally, we must not fear to follow the thread of Malcolm's evolution from the line of race struggle to the plane of race/class.

But we must study not in fear to keep us cowering in our corner of the cage, but study like a runaway memorizing an escape route through enemy territory that has been temporarily drawn in the dust.

Malcolm's books help us in all of this.

Unlike other leaders who were Malcolm's peers and who were great speakers but who left no written records of substance, Malcolm has gifted us with a legacy that stands as signposts in our development.

Moreover, Malcolm's books are part of the Third World literature of liberation and can rightfully be placed next to the works of Cabrall, Nyere, Ho, Guevera and others. Few others of our national leaders of the sixties meet that measure.

Malcolm challenged not just our actions but also our thinking, and in challenging us to think he inspired us in classic ways consistent with the best of African-American struggle.

To be for Malcolm X is to be for us.

I love Malcolm X.

DEATH IN THE FAMILY:
A MEMORY OF MALCOLM

Alfred Duckett

As I look back across the three score and five years I have been a visitor on this planet, I realize that I have enjoyed many blessings. Reviewing events since I was a teen-age kid, delivering a Black weekly to customers in Bedford-Stuyvesant and, later, bicycling around the borough of Brooklyn to place my paper - *The New York Age* - on newsstands - the communications business has been my passion. These days, I am doing a great deal of looking back as I work daily on my memoirs, *Confessions of a Ghostwriter: My Fifty-Year Love Affair With Language.*

That half century certainly has been exciting. One of my earliest and most lasting reminiscences related to writing occurred when there was a death in my family - the death of my grandmother. Alex Haley has observed that there is something very special about the empathy between grandparents and grandchildren. Grandparents, Haley declares, "sprinkle their grandchildren with stardust." Another observer has remarked that the affinity between grandchildren and grandparents is "only natural, considering the fact that they have a common enemy."

As a young boy, I had no understanding of such subtleties. I did not even know—not even understand the meaning of death. All I knew was that a warm and loving little old white-haired lady who loved me very much no longer lived with us— my schoolteacher mother and two sisters. They told me she had gone away, that she had left to take a long rest and dream a sweet dream. I understood with painful clarity that I would continue to miss her intensely.

The huge tree in the backyard of our one-family house was precious to me. It was my resting place and my refuge. I spent much of my time, stretched out on one of its broad branches, looking up into the clouds and watching the sun sail on its way to rest. The branch which served as my resting place was as comfortable as a cot. It was the perfect place to climb to when I wanted to dream, to be alone, to reflect. I spent several hours mind-searching for a way to express myself about my dear departed. I saw her again in memory, her smooth brown complexion, a loving smile, a delicious smell. I wondered how I would ever be happy again without her. At the depth of my private dilemma, I climbed down from my tree and on the bark of its trunk, I carved—painstakingly with a penknife—the first poem I remember creating. It read: "Grandma is dead. Now I am sad. If she would come back again, I would be glad."

Needless to say, the dear old lady never did return. As I grew up, I began to understand that the mysteries of birth and death and what comes in between—are as much of a puzzle to grown folk as they are to youngsters. But there have been deaths in my book of reminiscences which have influenced me mightily. One of these—another death in the family—was the assassination of Minister Malcolm X.

Because of the nature of my work, I had been keenly aware of the rise to eminence of Malcolm Little who had climbed up out of the pit of prison and dope dealing and street hawking of hot goods to become a Daniel for his people, a hot and angry and eloquently persuasive prophet who helped his brothers and sisters be aware that they could, indeed, fight back against the oppressive pressures of racism and persecution. I remember so clearly an incident in Harlem which Jimmy Hicks, now Editor of *The New York Voice*, describes with so much awe and admiration. It happened in Harlem after members of the Black Muslim Mosque headed by Malcolm had been apprehended by the police and were being held in the local stationhouse. Determined that his brothers receive justice, but not the Gestapo-type treatment often administered in our communities, Malcolm's quiet-mannered, well-dressed, highly

54

disciplined followers assembled in quiet, orderly fashion, in front of the precinct and waited outside with menacing calm while their leader, inside the stationhouse, argued for the release of his Muslim brothers. The police did not know how to handle the situation. They were afraid to begin a head-beating exercise as they did so frequently and with such savagery when dealing with one or two Blacks. There were many, too many bodies which, it was obvious, were led by a cool commander. The mass presence of this phalanx of citizen troops was threatening. Negotiations, not nightsticks, palaver, not pistols were the obvious answer to the dilemma of the bluecoats.

Inside the precinct, with all the power, persuasion and know-how of a professional advocate, the scholarly-looking Malcolm X argued for the rights of the prisoners. Finally, a deal was struck. In terms of this agreement with the police, Malcolm agreed to instruct his army to disperse. Within a matter of seconds after the agreement, the hundreds of Muslims who had crowded the street from one end to another, had disappeared at a simple sign from their leader. One of the police commanders, removing his cap and wiping his perspiring face, shook his head in sheer amazement and commented: "No one man should have that much power!" This police official did not say all he meant. He meant that no Black man should have the same kind of power that a police commander - who can, at a word, dismiss troops - enjoys.

I have seen Malcolm mesmerizing huge rallies where more police—usually mainly white—were monitoring events and marches. With his searing, almost sneering taunts and bold statements about the law and order troops in their midst, Malcolm levelled against them the heavy artillery of scorn and ridicule. He delighted his Black audiences with his daring. He was not ridiculing these law and order "guardians" for the sake of race-baiting. He was letting all of us know that we have no need to fear brutality and injustice when we are guilty of nothing but assembling and standing up for our God-given rights. He was heaping scorn on those blue uniforms to send the clear message to his people that so long as we call police, who should act as the paid servants of all peaceful people, "the man" - we shall acknowledge that we are less as men and women and indeed deserve to be treated as bad boys and girls. I loved him for that. Many of us did.

I also loved him for the power and magic of his speech, his sense of drama, the exquisite humor which he could invoke to let us see that we must stop being frightened of goons who could only justify their existence with billy clubs and guns.

I loved him for his teachings that we are connected to our heritage, that our forced importation into this country was not the beginning of our heritage, but a rude interruption. I loved him when he ridiculed Blacks who demanded what business Africa is of theirs. "Why should you be interested in Africa?" he would cry. "How can you ask such a question? Why you left your mind in Africa?"

I had a very personal reason for being indebted to Malcolm X which involved one moment when he spoke to me on the famed street meeting corner—125th Street and Seventh Avenue. This happened during the days when I had come back to Harlem as Executive Editor of *The New York Age*. A talented and dedicated disk jockey, Hal Jackson, who worked on Radio Station WLIB in those days when it was white-owned, was the target of an insidious campaign accusing him of accepting "payola" illegally for the purpose of promoting the records of certain artists. We, in Harlem, knew there was widespread acceptance of such under-the-table-benefits by whites in the field. We strongly believed in Hal's integrity and innocence on these charges. The late Rev. Oberia D. Dempsey, that intrepid man who fought dope and perversion of our youth in Harlem, and I were street corner speakers at a rally to defend Hal. We believed in his integrity. I spoke from some notes about the way the establishment exploited Black folk economically; the way that our sports heroes were used to help millionaires become richer, but were not good enough to be hired to do the lucrative commercials. It was a simple talk, a rallying cry for us, as Blacks, to protect and defend our own; to use our dollars in ways that would reward those who were treating us fairly and to withhold our financial support from those who displayed no gratitude or even recognition of our patronage. I did not know that Minister Malcolm was on the fringes of the crowd gathered there. But when the rally was ending, he walked over to me and held out his hand. "That speech was one of the best I've heard on this corner," he said smiling. If someone had handed me a large sum of money or some elaborate gift, I could not have been more grateful. For, in my opinion, then and now, Minister Malcolm was one of the most cogent, articulate and compelling communicators who has ever spoken for the cause of humanity. His ability to use sarcasm, his eloquence, his beautiful anger and rich humor—the derision he could pour upon phoney concepts—these made this man one of the great prophets in our history. Just as he inspired me, he inspired countless thousands of people around the globe.

Even, and perhaps, especially, in the manner of his death—in the assassination which certainly has a significance as yet unrevealed—he taught all of us willing to learn—that there is victory beyond the grave. As a close associate and writer for the late Dr. King, I was appalled to see in a television spectacular called "King" all the supposed negative aspects of the relationship between Dr. King and Malcolm X. This was one of the most monumental white lies of all time. Dr. King once confided to me, that Malcolm once said to the Dreamer—speaking of their common enemy—"I'm out there making the enemy scared to death so they'll have to come to you." Also, on one occasion, Minister Malcolm sent a clear message to racists that if they harmed a hair on Dr. King's head, he would see that they died. Ossie Davis, truly one of our most beautiful and articulate voices, called Malcolm at his funeral our "Shining Black Prince." There are so many people more equipped to reminisce about the marvel of Malcolm's life and crucifixion than I am. But I welcome the opportunity to say what little I can about this brother who rose up from the streets and prison life to become our sage and our saint. Truly, his passing was an epochal death in the family—the human family. Truly, his life instructs and inspires those of us who have the wisdom to appreciate him.

SCHOOLING MALCOLM:
MALCOLM LITTLE AND BLACK CULTURE DURING THE GOLDEN AGE OF JAZZ

Douglas Henry Daniels

In his youth Malcolm Little lindy-hopped to the swing bands and associated with musicians, but writers have not discussed this aspect of his adolescence. This is to some degree understandable. In the *Autobiography* Malcolm chronicled the degradation of his early years followed by his imprisonment, conversion, and abandonment of his life of crime, drugs, zoot suits, processed hair, jazz, and jitterbugging. "It was as though all of that life merely was back there, without any remaining effect or influence." Discussing his break with Elijah Muhammad, he said, "My life has always been one of changes." His evolution after leaving the Nation of Islam provided more evidence of a hiatus between his adolescence and his later development. His well-known abstinence and exemplary conduct help make understandable the conventional approach to these early years as simply the excesses of youth.[1]

Close examination of his account of his adolescence, however, reveals a pattern of continuity with his subsequent development in terms of his constant evolution while remaining devoted to the values of northern Black urban culture. Such an appraisal is necessary to understand Malcolm, for after all, one's formative years are linked to adult life. As Malcolm pointed out, "to understand [the life] of any person, his whole life, from birth, must be reviewed. All of our experiences fuse into our personality. Everything that ever happened to us is an ingredient." (150) In fact, the autobiography itself calls for such an analysis: seven chapters and one-third of the pages recount the phase in his life when Malcolm danced to swing bands and chronicled his life by the activities of the bands, the musicians, and the hit songs. There is a remarkable affirmation of Black culture and the humanity and potential of Afro-Americans throughout his autobiography, including the adolescent period. In this respect the work is a product of the sixties. Yet it rarely romanticizes this world, for Malcolm never lost sight of the way in which racism and oppression shaped values and choices. Malcolm championed the cause of Northern urban Afro-Americans and presented himself as a product of the popular culture of the big band era as well as of the prisons and Nation of Islam. He was as much at odds with the "respectable" culture of Euro-America as he was with the white racists. His affirmation of the jazz world was unique, insofar as other civil rights leaders either lacked a popular culture heritage or made no mention of it. Even scholars of the stature of W.E.B. DuBois, St. Clair Drake, and Horace Cayton neglected ragtime, jazz, and blues in their accounts of Black urban life. In this light Malcolm's autobiography is remarkable for spotlighting the importance of this music and Northern urban styles in Black culture and for drawing our attention to aesthetic and artistic considerations among a people that many characterized as basically lacking in culture if not altogether pathological.

The role of culture in Malcolm's development and thought has also been neglected. Close reading of the autobiography reveals a healthy cultural component to his adolescence which rarely receives attention. Malcolm presented an ever-changing identity in his development to emphasize his increasing sophistication and acquisition of Black cultural values. Significantly, his growth was encouraged by the constant counseling and coaching on the part of older and wiser Afro-Americans. The cool or hip philosophy that he learned accompanied his love of jazz music and dance in addition to the hustler activities for which he is chiefly known.[2]

Despite changes in his identity and behavior, Malcolm's

preference for jazz in the autobiography served to legitimate him with those urban dwellers who respected Black people and culture. Then too, it was a part of his demystification of the leadership of Negroes who aped the white elite and upheld its cultural values.[3]

Young Malcolm's fascination with Roxbury and Harlem night life needs to be seen in light of his geographic origins and early social life. In Michigan he never had the opportunity to live with large numbers of Afro-Americans or experience Black urban culture. After the death of his father, the family was primarily concerned with putting food on the table and staying together. When the family was separated, Malcolm lived with whites and attended school with them. When he left Michigan, he "couldn't dance a lick" — an indication of his lack of exposure to Black culture. (27)

From the time he arrived in Boston to live with his sister, Ella, Malcolm was primarily involved with Afro-Americans and their urban culture. His account of Boston and New York reflects a fascination with Black urban life as well as his naivete about the varieties of culture and class in Afro-America. The newcomer explained why he joined the society of poolroom attendants, shoeshine boys, numbers runners, waiters, and hustlers, people who idolized him after he became a race leader.

In the summer of 1940, Malcolm felt and appeared to his sister as "country." Like other newcomers, he set about changing himself to appear hip and cool — the first in what was to be a series of attempts to rid himself of an embarrassing past and keep in step with contemporary trends throughout his life. One obvious route to follow was that of the Hill elite, the Black residents of Roxbury who "acted and lived differently from any Black people I'd dreamed of." (40) They felt they were "cultured," "cultivated," and "dignified." The Hill people often owned homes and claimed they were professionals, "in government," "in finance," or "in law." They strode about "as if they were wearing top hats and cutaways." On the way to work they dressed "like ambassadors in black suits and white collars." (42) Their language was also stilted to the young Malcolm. They had "accents so phonied up that if you just heard them and didn't see them, you wouldn't even know they were Negroes." (59)

Although his sister preferred that he associate with them, Malcolm quickly concluded these were pretenders to status and high social position. Actually, the New England natives, the West Indians, and the descendants of the southern urban elite may very well have behaved in a manner that to them was natural.Such considerations never entered Malcolm's mind. He lumped New Englanders together with the "Southern strivers and scramblers" and West Indians, viewing them as "big-city" versions of bootblacks, janitors, cooks and maids he had seen in Lansing. He was amazed as much at their self-delusion as he was at their social snobbery. Malcolm rejected their society, claiming "my instincts were never...to feel myself any better than any other Negro." (43)

Instead he sought out the people whose status depended upon their own efforts in music, dance, sport, and hustling, and whose domain was within Black institutions such as restaurants, pool halls, bars, swing bands, and dance halls. Their behavior was rooted in Black cultural values that numerous Southern migrants and urban dwellers held dear. In "the town ghetto section...[which] seemed to hold a natural lure for me" Malcolm believed he could lead a life comparatively free of artifice and pretense. After all, these people had little contact with whites and were less concerned with proving their worth to them. This was particularly important to a youth whose family had been broken up and whose ambitions to be a lawyer had been frustrated by whites. In addition, the young Malcolm found this Black society "much more exciting...[and he] felt more relaxed among Negroes who were being their natural selves and not putting on airs." (42-

43) In Harlem, as well, Malcolm was attracted to what appeared to be a natural style of behaving in Small's Paradise, a famous club. Of the clientele and help, he said, "their manners seemed natural; they were not putting on airs." (72-73)

Malcolm's concern for natural behavior and manners reflected differences in style between the elite and other urban dwellers. The style in which Malcolm felt most comfortable was that of large numbers of poorer Blacks, recent migrants to cities, and hustlers, many of whom were united by their philosophy of cool and love of jazz and blues. While Malcolm rejected the Hill dwellers as pretentious, certainly pool players and loungers, racketeers, and card sharps are no more free of pretense and desires for higher status than anyone else. Nor was there anything natural about the zoot suit or conk hair style, both of which Malcolm eventually rejected.

Most significantly, it was these people, not the Hill dwellers, who befriended Malcolm, introduced him to their philosophy, put him at ease, counseled him, and claimed him as one of their own. Malcolm never forgot this, and it was part of the reason he was always their hero, before and after jail and, for that matter, in and out of the Nation of Islam. While Malcolm was later befriended by sympathetic whites and political and religious leaders from overseas, his first loyalty was always to those Black urbanites whose style made him feel comfortable in Roxbury and Harlem when he was a teenager. This continuity is remarkable testimony to the trust and affection he developed with these friends and their society.

Malcolm's increasing knowledge and exposure to Black cultural traditions found expression in the philosophy of cool that pervaded urban Afro-America. This aspect of Black culture has been traced to West African societies, where it functioned as an aesthetic and as a kind of philosophy useful for reconciling conflict. To be cool is to be self-possessed and in a state of equilibrium. It means avoiding the extremes of excitement and hot-headedness, on the one hand, and insensibility or immobility, on the other. One who has coolness can thus be a mediator and have a quieting, calming influence in society.[4]

In the Black urban communities of the north, coolness was clearly a stance or affectation as well as an indication one was knowledgeable. The new owner of a Cadillac whose number had hit was described as sitting parked in his car, "sharp as a tack, 'cooling it.' " (49) Coolness was also a worthwhile quality to set people at ease so they could be in the frame of mind to observe and learn. It became a by-word as Black urbanites drew attention to the necessity of being cool and calm. A friend told Malcolm, "Keep cool," the fellows would find him a job. (45) Malcolm told the shoeshine boy who was replacing him, " 'Keep cool' ...he'd soon catch on to the happenings." (58)

New arrivals and impulsive urban dwellers were schooled and protected from rash behavior in this fashion. Various people tried to cool Malcolm until he learned the required measure of wisdom and level-headedness. Older railroad men were afraid the intemperate Malcolm would be fired, for they quickly learned, " 'Man, you can't tell him nothing.' " (78) Malcolm lost a second job when, as a waiter in Small's, he acted rashly, asking an undercover vice squad man if he wanted a prostitute. Lionel Hampton's wife, Gladys, also tried to counsel him: " 'Calm down, Red.' " (111) New York's Black hustlers "took a liking" to Malcolm, "and knowing that I still was green by their terms soon began in a paternal way to 'straighten Red out.' " (186)

Malcolm's difficulties invariably resulted from his losing his cool. On impulse, he hit a friend's girl whom he could not calm down with words and consequently had to run for his life. (115) Another time he sat in a bar with his back to the door, even though he knew West Indian Archie was gunning for him, and his rival slipped up on him for a confrontation. In this instance, fortunately, Archie was calmed down and restrained by his friends. But eventually Malcolm's level-headedness saved his life, as when he refused to draw on an officer who had him covered by another detective at the time of his arrest. By learning to be calm and collected, Malcolm prevented trouble. During two close calls with the police, he used his head, flagging them down to ask for directions when they were seen approaching. The police assumed a criminal would never be so bold or so calculated as to approach the police if he had just committed a crime. When he set up the burglary ring, Malcolm took command by pretending to be crazy enough to risk his life before the gang's very eyes. He played Russian roulette, telling them the leader could not be someone who was afraid of death, but they did not know he had palmed the single bullet instead of putting it into the chamber. During his period as a follower of Elijah Muhammad, Malcolm's intemperate statements resulted in his suspension from public speaking engagements. His last words shortly before his assassination, significantly, showed how self-possessed he could be despite the frustrations of his last few weeks. An altercation that the assassins staged to divert attention was greeted with Malcolm's statement, " 'Hold it! Hold it! Don't get excited...Let's cool it, brothers—' " (434)

Northern Black urbanites of the swing era placed considerable emphasis on a cool style in speech, music, dance, dress, walk, manners, hustles, and other meaningful endeavors. They created an urban culture in addition to a unique style, both of which were quickly copied by whites—whether swing music, jump blues, jitterbugging, zoot suits, jive talk, or bop walks. Within this culture of the hip set or the cool world, each individual enjoyed the freedom of developing his own distinctive variant, although not everyone was expected to develop each area of life to the same degree.[5]

The first chapters of the autobiography are filled with examples of individuals striving to develop their own style and others who have done so. Malcolm's friend, Shorty, admired the leading alto stylist, Johnny Hodges. An unnamed Negro musician was remembered for smoking marijuana through a chicken bone. Sammy the Pimp was respected for his ability to detect a woman's weaknesses; West Indian Archie kept no written record of the numbers bets his clientele placed but everything stayed in his head. A shoeshine boy told a white man of plans to buy a Cadillac after hitting the numbers just to leave the job in greater style. Malcolm developed a reputation for craziness and for carrying several guns; Jumpsteady acquired his name from the style of his burglarizing; and numerous others — "Cadillac Drake" and "Dollarbill" had names calling attention to their singular exploits and claims to distinctiveness. (88-89)

After finding a job and before learning the more profound lessons of his new companions, Malcolm acquired the superficial aspects of the urban culture. These were the zoot suit, conk hair style, drug habits, and gambling. Zoot suits were the rage among Blacks in the cities, poorer whites in the immigrant districts, and Mexican-Americans in the southwest during the early forties. For Malcolm as well as other youth, it was a sign one had "arrived," that he was "cool." His new status had to be displayed publicly. Showing the suit off to its best advantage was known as " 'cooling it' — hat dangled, knees close together, feet wide apart, both index fingers jabbed toward the floor." Malcolm learned "the long coat and swinging chain and the Punjab pants were much more dramatic if you stood that way." (52) Proud of his new status as symbolized by the suit, he had himself photographed in this stance and sent copies airmail to Michigan.

Another step in Malcolm's acculturation to northern Black urban ways was acquisition of the conk. Eventually he came to realize it was only another initial stage and, ironically, a symbol of his newcomer status as much as the original hick suit and country hair style. "I was really a clown, but my ignorance made me think I was sharp." (78) Again he felt required to exhibit his new style as far as Michigan, where his appearance "staggered" Lansing residents. "I might have been taken as a man from Mars." (79) He kept this hair style until prison, but nonetheless Malcolm learned from various urbanites to change in other ways.

Recognition of the fact that, as a hustler, he must blend into the urban population caused him to abandon the zoot suit, especially after the non-too-subtle hints of a bar patron. A burglary ring executive presented Malcolm with "an expensive, dark blue suit, conservatively cut" — a token of his new status as well as a gift from someone who had his best interests at heart. (86) In his final stage of evolution as a hustler, Malcolm wrote, "I wouldn't have been caught dead in a zoot suit ... All of my suits were conservative. A banker might have worn my shoes." (136)

Malcolm learned to manipulate people through dress codes as he became increasingly sophisticated. When he received his draft notice, he "dragged out the wildest zoot suit in New York" and started to act crazy. He appeared at the induction center "costumed like an actor" and talking jive to officers and the psychiatrist. (104-107) Later he felt his brother, Reginald, whom Malcolm introduced to New York night life, needed to dress more conservatively. So Malcolm presented him with an overcoat and a suit with the message he himself had learned: "In order to get something you had to look as though you already had something." (104) While probably not adopted to mold opinion, Malcolm's wearing of the African shirts and Astrakhan cap of Black nationalists in the sixties reflected a concern with style that was meaningful to Afro-Americans.

Malcolm went to considerable length in the autobiography to give prominence to his absorption with popular music and dance. This represented another phase of his acculturation. For young Malcolm, Afro-American culture was primarily musical. The novelist, Ralph Ellison, expressed a similar opinion in recounting his childhood education in the Southwest in the twenties. Music and its close associate, dance, united musicians, dancers, and listeners into a society where each had a place and influenced one another in the dance halls, cabarets, schools, homes, wherever they met. Musicians and dancers were idolized, becoming models for proper behavior as well as for musical artistry. Dancers influenced popular taste in clothing by selecting suits, flared skirts, and low-heeled shoes that facilitated or enhanced movement during dancing. Together with musicians urban dwellers set the style in jive talk as well as music, dance, and dress. The jazz talk that fascinated Malcolm and northern Black city folk was in fact musical, having its own intonations and rhythms from the very music with which it was so closely associated.[6]

Shorty, Malcolm's poolroom friend, "was really serious about nothing except his music," and was waiting until he could form his own band. Besides greeting Malcolm as a homeboy when he learned they were both from Michigan, Shorty introduced him to the credit system for Negro consumers and directed him to a salesman in the store where Malcolm bought his zoot suit. They remained close friends. In fact, it was to help Shorty that Malcolm formed a burglary ring instead of going into the more solitary pursuit of gambling. Malcolm said of the alto saxophonist, "I really felt sorry for Shorty. The same old musician story. The so-called glamour of being a musician, earning just enough money so that after he paid rent and bought his reefers and food and other routine things, he had nothing left." (139)

Shorty was responsible for lining Malcolm up with his job at the Roseland State Ballroom, a site which was, in effect, Malcolm's first "class" in Black music, dance, and urban culture. He recalled he was so excited at the prospect of "being somewhere close to the greatest bands in the world" that he was "speechless" upon hearing of the opening, and went straight to the job without eating dinner. The music "transfixed him." As he shined shoes in the men's room, his "shine rag was popping to the beat of all their records, spinning in my head," and his feet would "suddenly break loose on their own and cut a few steps." "Music just wound me up." Malcolm claimed that "musicians never had had, anywhere, a greater shoeshine-boy fan than I was." (50) After he learned to dance, "I never missed a Roseland lindy-hop as long as I stayed in Boston." (59) The music and dance became so vital to his existence that he quit his job to have more time to dance.

In a subsequent job on the railroad, Malcolm had the opportunity to go to the citadel of Black culture at the time, which was Harlem. He visited Small's Paradise, which had a show, but this was not enough. Before the night was over he included the Apollo and the Savoy in his rounds. Malcolm was overwhelmed. The young dance fan "had never seen such feverheat dancing." "In one night...Harlem — had just about narcotized me." (75) He eventually moved out of Boston to be closer to the music and dance which increasingly figured in his life.

Working as a reefer peddler, Malcolm traveled with the swing bands, and he became more closely associated with the music and dance and his new heroes. Whenever he went to local dances, he would "show the country folks some plain and fancy lindy-hopping." (103) His association with the musicians and their behavior was such that "in most cases," he was thought to be one of the band. Small town fans mobbed him for autographs, and in Buffalo, Malcolm claimed, his suit was nearly torn off. As a result of his travels and sales, Malcolm "became known to almost every popular Negro musician around New York in 1944-45." (110)

Malcolm provided numerous examples of the recognition he was accorded by well-known musicians. When he made a particularly sensational display of dancing, "even Duke Ellington half raised up from his piano stool and bowed" in salute. (66) The only Black woman Malcolm dated in New

York was a singer, and they went to hear Billie Holiday, who knew them. The entertainer sang Malcolm's song, "the one she knew I always liked so," and visited at their table. (128) Malcolm's life had been threatened, and "Billie sensed something wrong with me." Moreover, she "knew that I was always high, but she knew me well enough to see that something else was wrong." Malcolm kept his distance, however, and his last mention of this event was when he claimed he had his picture taken with the two singers, huddled together with them at the table. (129-130)

A member of the in-group, Malcolm relished introducing his younger brother to Black music, his musician friends, and the urban culture. Among the notables who met Reginald were Billie Holiday, who "hugged him and called him 'baby brother,' " Lionel and Gladys Hampton, and the members of Hamp's band. The brothers went to the Savoy, the Apollo, "the night clubs and speakeasies, wherever Negroes played music," and had "wild times backstage." (110) Reginald became "a mad fan of musicians and music" and quit his job on the ships so he could stay in Harlem.

As further evidence of the importance music played in Malcolm's life, he relied on the hit songs and bands' appearances to chronicle these years. Erskine Hawkins' "Tuxedo Junction" and Slim Gaillard's and Slam Stewart's "Flat Foot Floogie" were hits while he was in Michigan. (28) He came to the Roseland to work when Benny Goodman was there and Peggy Lee had just joined him as a singer. (47) His first night in Harlem, Jay McShann, Dinah Washington, and Lionel Hampton performed at different night spots. Jimmy Rushing's "Sent for You Yesterday, Here You Come Today," Johnny Hodges' "Daydream," and Lionel Hampton's "Flyin' Home" were the rage during his stay in Boston and Harlem. (50,74)

At some time during this hustling life, Malcolm stopped dancing, perhaps about the same time he stopped wearing the zoot suit, because he mentions this together. (136)

Music and musicians still played an important role in his life and his imagination. When he had to leave New York for Boston, he spent a lot of time sleeping, but when awake, "I'd play records continuously...I would enjoy hours of floating, day dreaming, imagining conversations with my New York musician friends." (134)

The preference for jazz was not the only notable aspect of Malcolm and his friends' relations. His changing identity brings to light another important dimension of Black urban culture: the willingness of city dwellers to educate or "school" newcomers. This showed their concern and respect for Afro-Americans. Malcolm thanked the former Roseland shoeshine boy for showing him the ropes, " 'Man, you sure schooled me.' " (49) In Harlem, one of the Small brothers would stay late to help Malcolm learn his job, "teaching me things, for he didn't want to see me fired." The new employee "learned very quickly dozens of little things that could really ingratiate a new waiter with the cooks and bartenders." (80-81) School continued with the "customers who felt like talking as well as the bartenders and cooks." (81) "From a Harlem point of view, I couldn't have been in a more educational situation." (85)

Eventually Malcolm reciprocated. When his brother came to town he would "school him to what was happening" while in front of after hours clubs. (111) When he decided to start a burglary ring, Malcolm talked patiently with Shorty, his former instructor. "When I opened the subject of a hustle with Shorty, I started by first bringing him to agree with my concept — of which he was living proof — that only squares kept on believing they could ever get anything by slaving." (139) Malcolm put into operation the lessons he "had learned from some of the pros, and from my own experience, how important it was to be careful and plan to maximize success and mini-mize risk." (140)

Instances of these urban dwellers' concern for one another

abound. They help in finding jobs. Malcolm is told, " 'Some of the cats will turn you up a slave.' " Later Sammy thinks up a hustle for Malcolm when he loses his job at Small's, and Malcolm does the same for Reginald. They help in other ways. Sammy advises Malcolm to use his railroad identification to travel in order to stay out of New York "until the heat cools," and on a similar occasion calls for Shorty in Boston to come and get Malcolm. Then there are the numerous exchanges of money that indicated the extent to which they could count on mutual aid. Shorty offers Malcolm money, forcing him to take it when the homeboy claims he has a few dollars, until he finds a job. Sammy gives Malcolm a stake to start him in business. Malcolm, newly prosperous from his sales, immediately went to Boston to give Ella "a token of appreciation...for helping me when I had come from Lansing." (99) And she reciprocated when he was in prison and arranged for his transfer to a better facility.

Malcolm discovered greater humanity among the outcasts than among the so-called respectable citizens. He learned this when living in a building in which several prostitutes be-friended him. "It was chiefly the women who weren't prosti-tutes who taught me to be very distrustful of most women; there seemed to be a higher code of ethics and sisterliness among those prostitutes than among numerous ladies of the church." (91)

What is particularly striking about the early chapters is these bonds of friendship, trust, and humanity among people thought to be criminal or the victims of oppression. Despite the problems they faced as children and adults, Malcolm's family stuck by him in prison, introduced him to Islam, and provided for him in numerous ways. Close ties between Shorty, Sammy, Sophia, and Malcolm persist from 1940 to 1946. The prosti-tutes with whom he lived treated Malcolm like a "kid brother;" Billie Holiday greeted Reginald as "baby brother;" the patrons in Small's approach Malcolm in a "paternal way" when they counsel him. (91, 110, 86) And among the hustlers, there were people like the old-timer, Fewclothes, who maintained his dignity even though he depended on the charity of the people at Small's. (89)

These examples of humanity and warmth among the poor and oppressed are not merely romanticizations of ghetto life or the good old days, as it was Malcolm's main desire to portray the pernicious effects of racism and ghetto life. The sordid decline of many of his hustler companions during his imprisonment probably stays with the average reader more than the bonds of friendship. Nonetheless, his ability to recall several instances of concern and caring is ample testimony to their impact on Malcolm and the fact that he valued them several years later. Despite the risks of ghetto life, there was a measure of security and solidarity in this Black urban world just as there was in the Nation of Islam later.

Malcolm was in many ways a mirror or barometer of the changes Afro-American urbanites experienced from World War II to the sixties. Starting out as a country boy in the city, he was initiated into the popular as well as the superficial aspects of Black culture, learned to enlarge his limited opportunities through hustling and crime, and went through a remarkable spiritual conversion which enabled him to make a calculated analysis of the political arena from an international perspective. Initially, Black music provided the key to urban culture and to the homeboy's acceptance; then his display of sophistication in his hustles won him the respect he sought; later Islam, and finally Pan-Africanist thought provided paths of understanding. Malcolm's unique contribution to the process was his lending enormous popularity to each phase, swelling the ranks of the Black nationalists and the Pan-Africanists as he did the Muslims.

The changes in his identity brought into focus his singular ability to learn and, especially important, to benefit from the counsel and guidance of Afro-Americans— musicians, hustlers, Muslims, reporters, and politicians. Probably more than trained educators and scholars, these Afro-Americans contributed to Malcolm's growth and, ultimately, to the education of Black folk in the mid-twentieth century. Many educated people have difficulty understanding Malcolm's development and making a meaningful analysis of the Afro-American condition precisely because they lack a thorough grounding in Black culture, traditions, and experiences.

Outside observers have also misunderstood the emphasis on style in urban Afro-America. Malcolm, on the other hand, was aware of its connection with Afro-American aesthetics and traditions. He used his knowledge of styles of dress, for example, to popularize his ideals and perhaps to counter the pernicious effects of mass media. The zoot suit, the African national shirt, the conk, the afro and beard, the Astrakhan headgear after his trip overseas—every change signaled his changing ideals and growing sophistication.

Analyses of the role of culture in Malcolm's thought and growth invariably single out his statements concerning great African civilizations and the contributions of Islam and Arab culture. The popular music he discusses in his autobiography should help bring to the fore the importance of Afro-American cultural traditions in his evolution. This phase of Black culture has its well-known dissidents; Charles "Yardbird" Parker is the classic example. Musicians who became Muslims in the forties were also rebels in the cultural domain if not in the political. These dissidents, though often they did not develop a sophisticated political analysis, were heralds of the cultural changes in popular music, dress, and use of drugs that underpinned the rebellion of the sixties. These musicians were Malcolm's first teachers, initiating him into Black cultural traditions which he subsequently developed through his readings in history.[7]

In whatever phase we examine Malcolm, we find that he was

a messenger spreading the gospel of Black culture. When he spoke as a minister, he used the idiom and folklore of his respective audiences, relying upon his intimate knowledge of the music world, the streets, prisons, small towns, and large cities. After prison when he returned to his old haunts to find his hustler friends, he relied on the wire—that rather singular legacy of the Black oral tradition—to locate others as well as street talk to communicate when he found them. His knowledge of the varieties of the Black vernacular and Afro-American culture enhanced his ability to reach audiences and popularize the content of his religious and political programs.

Malcolm also relied upon his close acquaintance with Black culture to criticize certain Negro political and social leaders and to validate his own analysis. He drew upon the folk and urban traditions and styles which initially had put him at ease and which did the same for his listeners, allowing him to instruct them once their guard had been lowered. He stressed the cultural pretensions of the Negro elite as he strove to teach Afro-Americans to respect their indigenous traditions. He claimed that " 'Today's Uncle Tom doesn't wear a handkerchief on his head. This modern, twentieth-century Uncle Thomas now often wears a top hat.' " This Negro's cultural and stylistic preferences were foreign to most Afro-Americans and represented a conscious rejection of indigenous Black styles and values. " 'He's often the personification of culture and refinement...sometimes speaks with a Yale or Harvard accent...sometimes he is known as Professor, Doctor, Judge, and Reverend...a professional Negro...his profession is being a Negro for the white man.' " (243) In such statements Malcolm challenged the legitimacy of the Black elite, the traditional Negro professional class, and all those who wished to follow Euro-American cultural ideals.

Malcolm's presentation of his early days is far more than a classic case of ghetto pathology and self-hatred. It would be foolish to deny the existence of conflict and ambivalences about Black cultural heritage, however. Besides the conk Malcolm invariably stressed as a sign of self-hatred, there are other examples that provide us with clues about the urban dwellers' values. Freddie the shoeshine boy tells Malcolm, " 'Uncle Tom a little — white cats especially like that.' " (47) On the train, too, Malcolm and the workers "faked their Uncle Tomming to get bigger tips."(75) Significantly, in these instances and in others, such activity had an economic basis. One tommed with whites for the reason entertainers strove to please them — "to get their money." (87) The problem with such behavior is that it leads to self-delusion, for after a while one confuses the role with one's other identity.

Despite such ambivalences, Malcolm's contributions to the Black cultural renaissance of the sixties are amply documented by a close reading of his autobiography. In the future he will perhaps win recognition for these insights as much as for his political analysis. In fact, it is very likely he would not have analyzed the American political system in the way that he did without his immersion in Black music and urban culture during his formative years.

FOOTNOTES

1 Alex Haley, *The Autobiography of Malcolm X* (New York, 1981 paperback ed.), pp. 163, 408. Other citations to this work appear in the text.

2 John Horton, "Time and Cool People," Thomas Kochman (ed.), *Rappin' and Stylin' Out: Communication in Urban Black America* (Chicago, 1972), pp. 19-31; and Clyde Taylor, "The Language of Hip: From Africa to What's Happening Now," *First World* (January/February 1977), pp. 25-32 provide good analyses of the cool world and its values.

3 Betty Shabazz, "The Legacy of Malcolm X," *Ebony* (June 1969), pp. 178.

4 Robert Farris Thompson, "An Aesthetic of the Cool," *African Arts VII*

(Fall 1973), pp. 40ff.; "An Aesthetic of the Cool: West African Dance," *African Forum II* (Fall, 1966), pp. 85-102.

5 Milton "Mezz" Mezzrow and Bernard Wolfe, *Really the Blues* (New York, 1946), Cab Calloway, *Of Minnie the Moocher and Me* (New York, 1976), and Dan Burley, *Dan Burley's Original Handbook of Harlem Jive* (New York, 1944) recount this world.

6 Ron Welburn's Interview with Ralph Ellison, *The Grackle*, No. 4, pp. 77-78; on jive talk see footnote 5 and Robert S. Gold, *Jazz Talk* (New York, 1975). For his friendships with musicians as well as his activities as a hustler, Malcolm may have been exaggerating. Peter Goldman, *The Death and Life of Malcolm X* (New York, 1973), pp. 30-31 suggests this possibility, but then the question becomes why did Malcolm wish to give the impression he was close to the musicians?

7 Ross Russell, *Bird Lives! The High Life and Hard Times of Charlie (Yardbird) Parker* (New York, 1973).

PLAY

As Salaam Alaikum.

THE DEATH OF MALCOLM X

Amiri Baraka

Inner chambers of Uncle Sam Central. Men in Uncle Sam suits, some with long hats. The officers with fake beards to signify their rank. Some walking rapidly, some talking animatedly. Busy office...staging area for paramilitary operation.

Operating room. Crystal tank for body submersion. Drugged Negroes lying almost at random around the room, strapped to tables ... some nodding as if to come out of it.

Still another level downstairs. Slick bohemian...or arty nice white girls stroll in and out. Sign in place points out "Staging Area."

Still another level of facade of 1st level is mock coffee shop, beer joint, &c. Special exits, &c. Loud music...interracial couples, &c.

A tall white girl bends to kiss one drugged black figure on a stretcher, before he's wheeled away down the corridor to the operating room. Sign in corridor and outside hall reads "I.A.B.S." Institute for Advanced Black Studies.

Closeup of doctors operating on black boy, taking out his mindsoul, replacing it. They take out a black brain, substitute a white one for it.

Into a classroom. Just off staging area. Four Negroes stare glassy eyed at a blackboard upon which a white man in an Uncle Sam suit is writing certain instructions: "White is

Right" *(writes on board).*

INSTRUCTOR. Now repeat after me. *(They repeat)* White is
  Right. Right?
NEGROES. *(They answer)* Right!
INST. This is why the white man is so cool. This is why the
  white man is so great. *(He is pounding the board with
  his chalk for emphasis. The dazed Blacks repeat his
  phrases deadly.)*

In a war room of the staging area. Another white man is
pointing at plans for a large hotel. He points at each black
man in the room. "Now, 'A,' what do you do?"

A.   I stage the commotion.
WHITE MAN. "B"?
B.   I lead my men up the side hallway and through the
       front aisle, blasting after the first shot.
WHITE MAN. "C"?
C.   I get the four bodyguards out of the way, chasing the
       commotion with an order.

Back in the classroom they are showing movies of a black
caricature, now minstrel, now laughing insanely, now walking hunchbacked and meek, and whining over his fate. The
blacks in the audience boo and cheer, stomp their feet and
wring their hands. "Save us master...save us." Some of the
blacks are screaming, stomping, pounding on the chairs.
When the film is over these blacks will sit stiff with dazed
staring eyes.

War room. "O.K. A,B,C, let's hear it again." The white
instructor pointing with his stick.

The inner sanctum. The USam chiefs all dressed like

Sam...some of the higher ranked with crowns and scepters, or dressed like George Washington image with bandage wrapped around his head, some with Roman togas, some with Greek dress, a cave man, Vikings, Cortes' people, &c., set around discussing some issue quietly to themselves. While the chief, a young blond man with a neat goatee and sunglasses, is talking very animatedly on a television phone. He is talking to a fat dragon klansman. (If black and white film, suddenly switch to color to get the crimson, green, and gold gown.) The klansman sits in a luxuriously furnished room, surrounded by human bones and skeletons. Out a window behind him, the capitol bldg., or Washington Monument...some indication that it is Washington, D.C.

KLANSMAN. Well, what's holding things up then?

HP (HIPPY PRESIDENT). Authorization...but we'll get that probably this evening.

K.   You only got a little while, friend...you guys better not throw this chance away, don't you know. Lotta people counting on you. *(Smiles/leers)*

HP.   Don't worry...Don't worry...you just make sure your section has their end taken care of. You talk to the old man again?

K.   That ol' nigger's giving us trouble...but don't you worry about that. It'll be taken care of in the usual way. *(Rubs fingers   together signifying money.)* But you know all that...I seen one of your men hanging around me for the last week! *(Laughs)*

Classroom. A slide on the board of the Praxiteles...other Greek sculptures. Dazed blacks scream, "The beginning of thought...The beginning of Culture...God! God!"

INST. Yes...Yes...you're getting it now...*(Eyes wild w/joy, he and BLACKS foaming at the mouth)* Yes! Yr getting it now!! *(A group of half-naked white girls dance across the screen.)*

HP's office. Goateed man w/dark glasses kisses telescreen, as he turns it off. He turns from the screen and moves through the crowd, and all the assembled touch him. There are sexsenuous cries and love moans...i.e., from the Greek, the Roman, the Viking, &c.

Operating room. Closeup of scalpel cutting into black flesh...Faces of the assembled.

Tall lump faced man in a white 100 Stetson twirls rope in rodeo fashion, sings-"I'm a cracker / A dumb cracker too / I'm a cracker / A crackeroo." Repeats, ending with a long "Whoooooo," twirling rope, and leaping in the air. A crowd applauds. They hoist signs, of weird origins...e.g., one says "Hip White Stuff," another, "We want a lasting piece," dollar bills surrounding the lettering. One dazed black has a sign, "Please cool me out, white daddy." But most of the signs are admiring, e.g. "Hail to Lumpy Jaws." But in the background black protest signs are raised higher than all. "Freedom or Death" &c.

The door of an apartment is being beaten down. The man inside is dressed like an artist. His long haired, round eyeglassed woman sits on the bed, smoking nervously.
WOMAN.   Louis...what...???
LOUIS.   Get the weapons quickly! *(The door crashes in, BLACK MEN screaming with spears and swords crash through the door! They attack...On the wall of the room a picture of the man with dark glasses and goatee.)*

A white cop in a black neighborhood looks up suddenly, and

a garbage can is speeding for his head. He screams! Scene is repeated several times.

The klansman grinning...looking out his window at the capitol...talking on the phone. "Look, you ol' nigger...I told you you'd be taken care of. God damn it. Look, we can't talk like this...I know this is a special phone...but it's tapped too! When? Nigger sometimes you make me mad. You carry that poppycock of yours too far. That stuff's only for niggers. You keep them spirits to yrself." (*Laughs...grows quickly sullen...*) "Now look...you do what I tell you or you won't have any following at all. Yeh...that's right...He's got to die!"

War room. White man in US suit speaking. "All right you men go upstairs check your plans and routes, then get some sleep. You'll have to be on your way by 0900 tomorrow. There's a lot to do, before that." (On the wall a movie of lightskinned Negroes dancing a cotillion. On the arch where they pass under a huge sign says "Klugteufel Beer.") The black men raise their arms and shuffle woodenly out of the room, murmuring ecstatically.

Long rows of rolling stretchers, moving down a narrow corridor. Blacks to be operated on. Coming out to the other side of the operating room another long line...those already altered. Some stirring, smiling. Some blowing kisses. The attendants pointing.

The fat klansman with a blonde riding on his shoulders around the room. He has the top of his klansuit down, leaving his chest naked. She is licking his shoulder. She is screaming, "Giddyap, big pappa...giddyap!" He makes whinnying sounds, like a horse, and bucks stupidly.

Man w/goatee in his private office talking silently, on phone, curled in chair. Jazz playing quietly on box, in the walls. He rocks back and forth in an upholstered rocker. Puts phone down...buzzer sounds...he touches box at his elbow, "Yes"...(answer over intercom, "Col. Walters, sir.") "Send him in!" White man in US suit who was in war room comes in with papers, writing board, &c.

HP. Walters *(Extends hand)* sit down for Christ's sake.
WALTERS. Yes, sir.
HP. Well, what's happening, Walt?
W. Everything's together, sir. Project Sambo looks like it'll go off without a hitch.
HP. *(turns meditatively in chair, looking out window at Washington. Speaks quietly and with great satisfaction)* Yes...good...good...only one more project to be completed before the main one. Hummm, just one more possible hangup...
W. That ol' witchdoctor...
HP. Yes, but he's no problem at all, really. Our fat friend has the keys to his heart *(Rubs fingers together in money sign)*...that *(laughing)* and the Gandhi syndrome. *(W. laughs)*
HP. *(cont.)* But the quote followers unquote are ready? You've done yr job?
W. *(sobers)* Yes, sir. They're ready now to kill.
HP. Good...They'll have their chance very soon.

Main intelligence gathering room at USam Central. Huge room with television sets all over the walls. Radio voices beaming in. From far flung lands...murders...coups... treachery...jokes...murder voices cackling on and on. Men and women march around in Uncle Sam suits, tending to their business. Camera covers the room showing various information gathering activity. People reporting, rank delineation, &c.

Klansman sprawled on woman, talking, laughing. Image of capitol over his shoulder.

KLANSMAN. Yes, tomorrow's a big day, baby, a big day …Ha, ha, and in my humble capacity let's say, I'm a heavy contributor.

GIRL. *(laughs, squeals)*Oh,oh,oh, you're so important… I've never known anyone quite like you…you're Godlike…that's what I think…I think you're Godlike. (KLANSMAN *laughs, squirming and rocking his butt. His hand shoves out to turn on the television.*)

Television studio. A panel show is in progress…two white men seated flanking a tall hard jawed black man with rimless sunglasses. The black man is speaking…shaking his finger at the moderator and the tv cameras.

MALCOLM. No, finally it is the fact that you are evil. Evil. It is that simple fact that will animate the rest of the world against you! That simple alarming fact of your unredeemable evil. You are all disqualified as human beings, *(Voice rises sharply)* disqualified by your inhuman acts …

Klansman's bedroom. *(Malcolm's voice is droning over the television, "by your inhuman acts…your filth and your evil.")* Klansman looks up at tv, stares hard at the words and the (unseen) face, his face twisted in a leering grimace, then he begins to laugh.

KLANSMAN. Hahaha…yr right nigger…yr right…hahaha…by our evil…hahaha…but what good will it do you…*(laughing hysterically…his female companion follows with highpitched shrieks.)*

Out the window, down the street. A crowd of civil rights marchers, the Negroes impeccably clad. They are chanting mindlessly, "LET US BE AMERICANS." It is an integrated picket line, fat white ladies with sparkling necklaces...priests and ministers ogling each other. They are led by a tall "distinguished" looking Negro with greying temples. He is walking in long gallant strides, turning his head from one side to the other to take in the applause (and abuse). The streets are lined with white people.

Shots of the windows of the official offices. Laughing fat faces, pointing and ridiculous. There is music with the marchers. Some of the marchers are singing "WE SHALL BE WHITE" in a spiritual vein..."WE SHALL BE WHITE"...they walk down the street with a militancy...but bereft of humanity. Beautiful automatons. "WE SHALL ALL BE WHITE." The rich ladies scream with laughter. Bohemians promenade. Cops line both sides of the street, some snarling and baring their teeth. Most of the people that line the streets are in USam suits and cop suits. As the crowd of marchers passes down the street chanting their slogan, we begin to see a crowd of policemen and plainclothesmen gathering slowly at a point in advance of the marchers. Some of the marchers we recognize from the classroom or the operating room. And as the procession moves down the street...employees of the USam bureau are going in and out. Cops and plainclothesmen stop marchers...They kneel and begin to pray. "Oh, white Northamerican God, help us...help us to be like you and your loved ones." The marchers repeat their whines. They begin to weep en masse, the leader bawling like a baby. All praying, hands to chin, rolling their eyes. The policemen's clubs and billies beating the demonstrators in agonizing slow motion. Camera moves away from the scene, widening the shot, to include the whole ritual-like melee.

Television studio. Guards standing around in presence of a speaker…Secret Service types. A voice announces, "Ladies and gentlemen the President of the United States." Assembled people applaud. Closeup of a handpuppet speaking into the cameras, gesturing, like a speaker, like a president making a state of the union message, or at an official press conference.

PRESIDENT. *(in cowboy accent)* "Friends, violence…*(Aside)* to us…hahaha, is not the answer. The only answer is the law, and law abiding citizens. Rome wasn't…hahaha…built in a day. *(Aside)* Nor without slaves…hahaha…We will have an equitable society, a beautiful society, but it must be built through the laws of the land…by strengthening those laws not marching in defiance of them!! America is a beautiful country…a beautiful idea…America will exist forever.

(Applause from people out on the street, watching tv's in an appliance store window.)

Police beating the marchers. The greyhaired man stands, untouched, at the center of the melee. He is beatified, a red white and blue halo appears illuminating around his head. Now he turns and addresses the embroiled marchers. With his arms still spread, as if to bless them, he says in the midst of the turmoil: "Go home my children…we have proven our point, that love is stronger that hate!" People's heads are being cracked open…women are wrestling with policemen. The greyhaired man goes on: "Go home, my children…we have beaten them, I say, we are this day blessed! We will be white…We will be whiter than them" (points at the policemen; at the white crowd). "Whiter, much whiter." He says the last words into a wrist radio.
Instructor in classroom, white man in war room, bearded

pres., klansman, all pick up on what's being said, through speakers in their offices. Come to focus closeup of bearded man and klansman, each with their different laughter. Final image of handpuppet, listening to wrist radio, breaking up with weird puppet laughter.

Night: The sky is a monstrous American flag, illuminated as if in neon, the red, the white, the blue...the stars, in the flag, glowing.
Underneath, an occasional scream or bomb. To break up the silence with the character of a quietly hysterical American night. The feeling must be given of unbelievable agonies going on...above them, the shrill laughter. The occasional burst of fire.

Dawn to morning: the flag of American sky grows dim and breaks up into white clouds. It is Sunday morning. A calm over the cities. Washington/New York. We see white people going to church, starched and stiff, the black people going into their churches. The otherwise quiet streets. Shops, businesses closed.
At the USam offices, however, people are moving back and forth. There is an anteroom, where the men take off their outside clothes, revealing USam suits. The women in another chamber, the top hats collapsible ones they take out of their pockets or pull out of the lockers.

Airplane interior. The dazed Negroes sitting inside being talked to by the war room officer, "Now let's go over the details one more time."

ATTENDANT. Sir, we'll be in New York in 15 minutes.
INSTRUCTOR. All right men, check your weapons...and go
        over your assignments for me one more time.
NEGROES. "I get the guards out of the way." "I stage the

commotion." "I lead my men up the side hallway and through the front aisle, blasting after the first shot." After the briefing…attendant comes back, "5 minutes."

INST. O.K.…uh…men. *(Loudspeaker starts playing Star Spangled Banner. NEGROES fall on floor licking the WHITE MAN's shoes one at a time, in perfect order. The plane, seen from the outside, speeds on.)*

As the plane lands, and the men get out and are picked up in cars, which speed off towards the city, the tall bearded black man with the rimless glasses is just getting out of bed. Knock on the door of the room.

MALCOLM. Come.

S. *(M's aide comes in)* Morning.

M. Morning.

S. Sir, we've got to get started…we're sort of running behind schedule…as it is.

M. O.K., O.K., my egg and juice ready *(Calling out into the hall)*??

WIFE'S VOICE *(from out in the hall)* Sure they're ready. The kids are up too. Only thing not functioning in here is you. *(Laughs. Voices of kids, "Daddy's up…daddy's awake…daddy's awake.")*

S. We're supposed to be at the hall in about an hour. It's 30 minutes just to get to the city.

M. Yeh…yeh…we'll make it. *(Starts to get himself together.)* Say, what's happening in the world this morning?

S. *(w/newspaper)* Same ol'. Same ol'. Charles still knocking people off. People still not together…makes the meatball's attitude much safer and stronger.

M. And much more deadly. Well today is a historic date, of some kind. Got a lot of things to say this morning.

(Laughs, dressing)

S.   *(laughs)* I know. I know.

House bell rings…Wife calls out, "Malcolm, Price and the others are here."

M.   O.K.

S.   I'll see to them.

M.   *(S exits, M humming to himself, tying tie &c., looking over a speech he is to give at the ballroom…just a few words are audible)* "…is mass murderer. I got proof." *(Laughs.)* Hmmm…that ought to shake up a whole lot of devils. Shake 'em very hard.

S.   *(calling from next room)* Brother Malcolm, we gonna be late…*(Laughs)* again.

M.   *(finishing up going over his speech)* Just keeping the stereotype, brother, that's all, just keeping the stereotype. *(He enters dining room, six MEN sitting around the table stand when he enters.)*

ALL.   Greetings, Bro. M. Morning.

M.   Sit Sit…get that grease and let's split. *(All laugh and begin eating.)*

BEARDED HP. *(talking on phone)* Yes…yes…that is right. About 45 minutes, unless he's late. Right. It's done. *(Turns away from phone, punches intercom)* Ross, turn on the television to any news broadcast…let me know at once if anything…uh…important happens.

ROSS. Yes, sir.

Fat Klansman disturbed by phone…waddles out of bed…girl in bed moaning about the disturbance…"Oh, God…baby, why do you have to leave me?"

KLANSMAN. Bizness…I trust…bizness *(Picks up phone).* Yeh…of course…it's taken care of in one half hour, I

92

get here…unless the nigger's late. I *(Laughs)*. Right *(Laughs)*. The old man is O.K….I fixed it. It's up to yr people now. Right! *(Hangs up phone. Calls to GIRL)* GobbleGobble…GobbleGobble…

GIRL. Yes, God, baby.

K.   Turn on the tv…get a news program. Something nice is gonna happen in a few minutes. A historic event.

G.   Wheeee…oh, baby…that's what I like about you…yr in on everything.

Elegant inner office of elegant mansion. Stacks of bank notes lie all over the place, though neatly stacked. Gold bullion on the floor. A portrait of Uncle Sam dressed in gold. Fat bald white banker sits surrounded by money, talking on phone.

BANKER.   Looter, here. Yes…everything in readiness?? Yes, O.K. I have my suit pressed for the occasion. A little party at my place afterwards…Yes…wear your good clothes…Haha…the rite goes on, eh? Good…O.K. O.K. *(Knock at the door)* O.K., got to leave now; right…15 or so minutes, huh?? O.K. right…see you this evening…the good Lord willing. *(Hangs up)* Come in. (SERVANT *comes in dragging huge sack of money*) Just drop it in the corner…no, better…just dump it on the floor. *(Dumps gold coins on floor)* Beautiful…beautiful. That'll be all. *(Room is furnished like study, library, rumpus room, with trophies, black man's shrunken head like Patrice Lumumba on wall)* Beautiful. *(Goes, looking at his watch, to turn on tv, then goes back and sprawls in the gold, wallowing drunkenly.)*

The greyhaired Negro standing before a banquet audience. A huge white man handing him an award; says, as he hands it to

93

him, "For Meritorious Service." The assembled white audience applauds and cheers.

The Audubon Ballroom. Black people going in, white police around. We see the four black traitors arrive separately, one looks at one of the policemen, significantly. M's cars arrive. The men get out walking casually in front and in back of him. M turns to make sure his wife and children get out and are walking beside him.

M.   Beautiful...Beautiful day...The sun is strong medicine.

(*People greet him:* "Good afternoon, Brother M.")

M.   Good to see you, on this beautiful day.

(*One old lady gives him flowers and a sudden kiss on the cheek.*)

M.   (*jokingly*) Easy madam, my wife's here. (*All laugh...He goes in, greeting people.*)

The greyhaired Negro is receiving his award. The crowd applauds. His wife comes to embrace him. She is dressed in a civil war ball gown. Closeup of the crowd applauding each other. The other speakers on the stage, the Negro grinning from ear to ear. The award he has received is a life sized watermelon made of precious stones and gold.

At klansman's. Km has his klan suit on, also, the girl has taken from a newly unwrapped box, two dresses...one is the green and maroon feminine pairing of his costume, another dress made out of an American flag, just like the USam suits.

94

They have been practicing putting on a small tee. The fat man is putting, now watching tv. At this point the screen (which does not have to be seen): "We interrupt this program to bring you a special bulletin..."

Banker's home. The banker spins on his heel, while counting the money...at the same announcement.

Audubon. M is walking onto the stage...people are being seated. His bodyguard has formed where they are supposed to. Four in front of the stage. Stationed in balcony, and at back of hall. The assembled applaud as M approaches the podium.

Bearded HP and his staff sit now, in front of tv, sipping drinks. Instructor and his staff and war room staff sit, joking quietly, taciturn and tensed. Office of USam: People aware more or less of something impending momentarily. The US uniforms pausing, perhaps, to whisper to each other, keeping eyes on clock, some eyeing television screens, or listening to small radios...still going through the motions of their work.

Empty war room. W/black board upon which is written OPERATION SAMBO, also times; operators' code names; trans instructions; ops officer in charge, &c.

Audubon. Also from radios, USam tv's. M is speaking: "They are evil people because they benefit by being evil...or they think they benefit...finally, they will not benefit by it at all. Not at all. (Applause.) We speak of revolution and don't even know what it is. A revolution means land. (Audience responds with "Speak Brother," "Go ahead"..."Amen.") A revolution also means bloodshed. There is no revolution without bloodshed."

(The man in the middle of the hall begins a rumble…M's bodyguards move forward on a signal from one man who seems to be in Malcolm's guard. The killers in the audience start to move. He holds up his hands…in peace.)

M.   Oh, O.K., cool it brothers…everything's gonna be O.K.
(The shooting begins. The killers move up the aisles, blasting away…Closeup of Malcolm's face. He grabs his chest. People scream.)

The news on tv, in all the rooms. The white men howling with laughter or snickering, or grinning half embarrassed at their victory. As the news is announced all the ofays begin to change clothes, and put on Uncle Sam suits, top hats and chin beards. The banker begins to call people about his party.

Malcolm is falling. People screaming. The assassins disappearing in a prearranged manner. Into cars…to an abandoned part of town…since it is Sunday. Then to a waiting helicopter and off.

Malcolm's body in closeup. The bullets hitting him again, him clutching his chest.

Now a shot of black people (and Africans and Asians and Latinamericans) clutching their breasts, as if shot, at the same time.

The greyhaired Negro is finishing buttoning on his USam suit. The audience still applauding.

Malcolm dead on floor with weeping hysterical mourners.

We hear the tv announcer: "Today black extremist Malcolm X was killed by his own violence."

Klansman is laughing, fingering the girl's snatch, &c.

Last image is of all the featured ofays together at a party in USam suits, celebrating and making jokes, later going through a weird historic ritual, with the Viking, Conquistador, Caveman, Roman, Greek, leading a slow weird dance as they put on USam suits, making growling unintelligible noises, but ending each phrase rhythmically with "White!" "White!" "White!!" "White!!" &c.

-Black-

SELECTED BIBLIOGRAPHY ON MALCOLM X

This Bibliography is presented as it appeared in the original *Tribute*. A wealth of material has subsequently been published.

Books

Breitman, George. *The Last Year of Malcolm X*. New York: Schocken Books, 1967.

Clarke, John Henrik (ed.) *Malcolm X: The Man and His Times*. New York: The Macmillan Company, 1969. 21 Black writers on the most charismatic and pivotal figure in Afro-American history.

Epps, Archie (ed.). *The Speeches of Malcolm X at Harvard*. New York: William Morrow, 1968.

Goldman, Peter. *The Death and Life of Malcolm X*. New York: Harper & Row, 1974.

Malcolm X (with the assistance of Alex Haley). *The Autobiography of Malcolm X*. New York: Grove Press, 1965.

Malcolm X. *By Any Means Necessary*. New York: Pathfinder Press, 1970.

Malcolm X Speaks. New York: Grove Press, 1965.

Malcolm X. *The End of White World Supremacy*. New York: Merlin House, 1971.

Malcolm X on Afro-American History. New York: Pathfinder Press, 1967.

Randall, Dudley, and Burroughs, Margaret B. *For Malcolm*. Detroit: Broadside Press, 1966.

Smith, Baxter; Porter, Herman; Breitman, George. *The Assassination of Malcolm X*. New York: Pathfinder Press, 1976.

Wolfenstein, Eugene Victor. *The Victims of Democracy: Malcolm X and the Black Revolution*. Berkeley: University of California Press, 1981.

Periodicals

Adams, Alvin. "Malcolm X 'Seemed Sincere' About Helping Cause: Mrs. King." *Jet*, March 11, 1965.

Allen, Robert. "Malcolm X: 2/21/65." *Village Voice*, February 17, 1966.

Black, Pearl. "Malcolm X Returns." *Liberator*, January, 1965. (Report of the first OAAU rally held after Malcolm's second return from Africa, on November 29, 1964.)

Capouya, Emile. "A Brief Return from Mecca." *Saturday Review*, November 29, 1965. (An intellectual's report of how his opinion of Malcolm changed.)

Cleage, Jr., Albert. "The Malcolm X Myth." *Liberator*, June 1967.

Davis, Ossie. "Why I Eulogized Malcolm X." *Negro Digest,* February 1966.

Dunayevskaya, Raya. "Malcolm X and 'Old Radicals.' " *News and Letters* (Detroit), April 1964.

Flick, Hank. "A Question of Identity: Malcolm X's Use of Religious Themes as a Means for Developing a Black Identity." *The Negro Educational Review,* V. 31, #3, July-October 1980.

Gardner, Jigs. "The Murder of Malcolm X." *Monthly Review*, April 1965.

Hall, Gordon D. "Malcolm X: The Man and the Myth." *Boston Sunday Herald,* February 28, 1965.

Handler, M.S. "Malcolm X Splits with Muhammad." *New York Times,* March 9, 1964.

Henry, Laurence and Richard. "Malcolm X." *Now*, March-April 1966.

Herman, David. "3,000 Cheer Malcolm X at Opening Rally in Harlem." *The Militant*, March 30, 1964.
—. "Malcolm X Details Black Nationalist Views." *The Militant*, April 20, 1964.
—. "Malcolm X Back from Africa-Urges Black United Front," *The Militant,* June 1, 1964.

Holt, Len. "Malcolm X: The Mirror." *Liberator*, February 1966.

Illo, John. "The Rhetoric of Malcolm X." *Columbia University Forum*, Spring 1966.

Jones, Theodore. "Malcolm X Knew He Was a 'Marked Man.' " *New York Times,* February 22, 1965. (An interview three days before the assassination.)

Karlengu, Maulana. "Malcolm and the Messenger: Beyond

Psychological Assumptions to Political Analysis." *Black News*, Summer 1982, Uruhu Sassa, Brooklyn.

Kempton, Murray. "Malcolm X." *Spectator* (London), February 26, 1965.

Lincoln, Eric C. "The Meaning of Malcolm X." *Christian Century*, April 7, 1965.

Major, Clarence. "Malcolm the Martyr." *Negro Digest,* December 1966.

Massaquoi, Hans J. "Mystery of Malcolm X." *Ebony*, September 1964.

McGill, Ralph. "Essay on Malcolm X and Black Muslims." *Detroit News,* March 3, 1965.

McManus, Jane. "The Outlook of Malcolm X." *National Guardian,* April 18, 1964.

Miller, Roland. "Malcolm X: The Final Interview." *Flamingo*, Ghana edition, June 1965.

Morrison, Allan. "Who Killed Malcolm X?" *Ebony,* October 1965.

Neal, Lawrence P. "A Reply to Bayard Rustin—The Internal Revolution." *Liberator*, July 1965.

Norden, Eric. "Who Killed Malcolm X?" *The Realist*, February 1967.

Parks, Gordon. "Violent End of the Man Called Malcolm X." *Life*, March 5, 1965.

Price, William A. "Malcolm's Death Spotlights Gap Between Negro and White." *National Guardian*, March 6, 1965.

Robeson, Eslanda. "Malcolm X's Funeral, Dignity and Brotherhood." *Baltimore Afro-American*, March 20, 1965.

Robinson, Louie. "Redd Foxx—Crown Prince of Clowns." *Ebony*, April 1967.

Schrath, R.A. "Malcolm X Is Alive." *America*, April 22, 1967.

Schrath, R.A. "The Pilgrimage of Malcolm X." *Catholic World*, September 1967.

Sevaile, William. "The Assassination of Malcolm X: The View from Home and Abroad." *Afro-Americans in New York Life and History*, January 1981.

Shabazz, Betty. "The Legacy of Malcolm X." *Ebony*, June 1969.

Sheppard, Barry. "Interview With Malcolm X." Interviewed by Jack Barnes. *Young Socialist*, March-April 1965.

Smith, Adeyemi. "Malcolm On Islam and Social Justice." *African Mirror*, July 1980.

Smith, Adeyemi. "Malik Shabazz: The Man History Has Forgotten." *African Mirror*, February-March 1979.

Snellings, Rolland. "Malcolm X As International Statesman." *Liberator*, February 1966.

Spellman, A.B. "Interview with Malcolm X." *Monthly Review*, May 1964.

Stone, I.F. "The Pilgrimage of Malcolm X." *New York Review of Books,* November 11, 1965.

Southwick, Albert. "Malcolm X: Charismatic Demagogue." *Christian Century,* June 5, 1963.

Walker, Wyatt Tee. "Nothing But a Man." *Negro Digest,* August 1965.

Warde, William F. "The Life and Death of Malcolm X." *International Socialist Review,* Vol. 26, Spring 1965.

Wechsler, James A. "Malcolm X and the Death of Rev. Klunder." *New York Post,* April 13, 1964.

Warren, Robert P. "Malcolm X: Mission and Meaning." *Yale Review,* December 1966.

Wiley, Charles W. "Who Was Malcolm X?" *National Review,* March 23, 1965.

Young, Whitney, Jr. "Malcolm's Death Solves Nothing." *New York World Telegram and Sun,* February 25, 1965.

***

"Interview With Malcolm X." *Young Socialist,* March-April 1965.

"Lesson of Malcolm X." (Editorial) *Saturday Evening Post,* September 12, 1964.

"Malcolm X." *New Statesman,* June 1964.

"Malcolm X Splits with Muhammad." *The New York Times* account of the split, March 9, 1964.

Revolutionary Action Movement (RAM). "Why Malcolm X Died." *Liberator,* April 1965.

"Tragedy of Malcolm X." *America*, March 6, 1965.

Plays

"El Hajj Malik El-Shabazz," by N.R. Davidson, Jr. (Presented at the Jamaica Arts Center, Jamaica, NY, Summer 1982)

"Chickens Come Home to Roost," by Lawrence Holder (Presented at the New Federal Theatre, New York City, Spring 1981)

Long Playing Records

Ballots or Bullets. Jamie Guyden Distributing Corp., 919 North Broad Street, Philadelphia, Pa.

Malcolm X Speaks Again. Twenty Grand Records, New York, 1965.

Message to the Grass Roots. Afro-American Broadcasting Co., Detroit, 1965.

PROFILES

Comments on the authors' activities have been updated wherever possible, and in no manner reflect all their individual accomplishments.

AMIRI BARAKA (LeRoi Jones) is one of the most versatile writers in America. He has written poetry, plays, fiction and essays. His works include *Blues People*; *Raise Race Rays Raze*; *The System of Dante's Hell*; *Dutchman and The Slave*; *Four Revolutionary Plays*, *Daggers and Javelins: Essays* , and *Selected Poetry of Amiri Baraka*. *The Autobiography of Leroi Jones/Amiri Baraka* was published in 1984 (Freundlich).

GWENDOLYN BROOKS has been Poet Laureate of Illinois since 1968. Among her awards are the Pulitzer Prize for Poetry, and the American Academy of Arts and Letters award. In 1989, she received the Poetry Society of America's Frost Medal. She is the author of over twenty books, the most recent of which is *Children Coming Home* (1991) published by the David Company. She holds the Gwendolyn Brooks Chair in Black Literature and Creative Writing at Chicago State University.

JOHN HENRIK CLARKE is an historian, writer and educator. His works include *Reclaiming the Lost African Heritage*; *Rebellion in Rhyme (Poetry)*; and two anthologies on Harlem - *Harlem, a Community in Transition* and *Harlem, USA*. He has been Associate Editor of *Freedomways Magazine*.

DOUGLAS HENRY DANIELS is a Professor at the University of California, at Santa Barbara, where he teaches in the Department for Black Studies. Among his works is *Pioneer Urbanites: A Cultural and Social History of Black San Francisco* (University of California Press). His biography on Lester Young will be published in the Spring of 1993 by Norton Press.

ALFRED DUCKETT was a journalist, editor, speech-writer, author. He wrote for the Black Press in such publications as *Ebony*, *Negro Digest*, *Tan Magazine* (of which he was also the Executive Director), and Associated Negro Press International.

JAMES JENNINGS is Professor of Political Science, and Director of the William M. Trotter Institute at the University of Massachusetts, Boston. His recent publications include *The Politics of Black Empowerment* (Wayne State University Press), *Race, Politics and Economic Development: Community Perspectives* (Verso Press).

J.E.M. JONES is a writer and poet. *Travelin' on Faith, Travelin' on Credit,* a collection of her works, was published in 1982.

C. ERIC LINCOLN, author of *The Black Muslims in America*, is currently Professor of Religion and Culture at Duke University. His books include *The Black Church in the African-American Experience* (1991), *Is Anybody Listening to Black America?* and *The Negro Pilgrimage in America*.

D.H. MELHEM is a poet, author, critic, and playwright, who has published three books of poetry. Her critical work includes *Gwendolyn Brooks: Poetry and the Heroic Voice* and *Heroism in the New Black Poetry: Introduction and Interviews*, which won an American Book Award in 1991.

KALAMU YA SALAAM was the Editor of the *Black Collegian*. He is a writer and poet, and his works have appeared in the *Black Scholar*, *First World*, *National Leader*, *In These Times* and others. He is the author of *Our Women Keep Our Sky From Falling: Six Essays In Support Of Smash Sexism/ Develop Women* (Nkombo Press).

SONIA SANCHEZ is the author of many books including *Homecoming, It's A New Day, Lovepoem,* and *I've Been A Woman: New and Selected Poems* (Black Scholar Press). She has edited *We Be Word Sorcerers: Twenty-Five Short Stories by Black Americans* (Bantam). She has been a Contributing Editor of *Black Scholar,* and is Associate Professor at Temple University in Philadelphia, in the English Department. In addition she is a member of the literature panel, Pennsylvania Council of the Arts.

JUAN VILLEGAS is a writer, poet and actor. He has been published in numerous anthologies, and lectured at several colleges and universities in the northeast. He is currently involved in a performance group in New York City, *Wise Guise.*

LOUIS C. YOUNG, JR. was the founder of the Scribe School and Scribe Editorial Service, a professional writing and research firm. He is also a free-lance writer whose articles have appeared in *Elan, Essence, Black Enterprise, Players* and others.

ADEMOLA OLUGEBEFOLA has been involved in the arts of song, music, and theatrical direction on the road to becoming one of the most respected and inventive catalysts in the contemporary Black Arts Movement. Ademola's work encompasses painting (oil, watercolor, acrylic), woodcuts, sculpture, drawing (publication design and layout, and illustration) and interior design. Recently published by Grinnell Collection is *Ademola Olugebefola: Twenty-five Years of Classics in American Art 1965-1990.*

JAMES B. GWYNNE is a teacher and writer, living in New York City. He is currently working on a biography of Arturo Alonso Schomburg.

EPILOGUE

Know that the LORD is GOD; He has made us and we are His own, His people, the flock which He shepherds. Enter His gates with thanksgiving and His courts with praise. Give thanks to Him and bless His name; for the LORD is good and His love is everlasting, His constancy endures to all generations.

Psalms 100: 3-5

A man may say, "I am in the light;" but if he hates his brother, he is still in the dark. Only the man who loves his brother dwells in light: there is nothing to make him stumble. But one who hates his brother is in darkness; he walks in the dark and has no idea where he is going, because the darkness has made him blind.

John 1: 9-11

They seek to extinguish the light of God with their mouths; but God will perfect His light, much as the unbelievers may dislike it.

The Koran 61:8

HELP STOP THE KLAN